People, Promise and Community

*A Practical Guide to Creating
and Sustaining Small Communities of Faith*

by Harriet Burke, Bill Edens,
Ken McGuire and Maggie Stapp

Paulist Press
New York and Mahwah, N.J.

Scripture selections are taken from the *New American Bible* Copyright © 1970 by the Confraternity of Christian Doctrine, Washington, D.C. and are used with permission. All rights reserved.

Book design by Nighthawk Design.

Cover design by Moe Berman.

Copyright © 1997 by Harriet Burke

Library of Congress Cataloging-in-Publication Data

People, promise, and community / by Harriet Burke... [et al.].
    p. cm.
   Includes bibliographical references.
   ISBN 0-8091-3665-1 (alk. paper)
   1. Church group work. I. Burke, Harriet, 1931–
BV652.2.P46 1996
253'.7—dc20
                                           96-41354
                                             CIP

Published by Paulist Press
997 Macarthur Boulevard
Mahwah, New Jersey 07430

Printed and bound in the
United States of America

CONTENTS

ACKNOWLEDGMENTS

Grateful acknowledgment is made here for permission to reprint the following copyrighted materials:

I Begin to See, by Thomas M. Corry, 1990. Copyright Long Run Productions, P.O. Box 152, Santa Barbara, CA 93116.

Making Friends with Yourself, by Leo P. Rock, S.J., 1990. Copyright Paulist Press, 997 Macarthur Boulevard, Mahwah, NJ 07430.

Prayers for a Planetary Pilgrim, Lenten Psalm of the Royal Road, by Edward Hays, 1989. Copyright Forest of Peace Publishing, Inc., 251 Muncie Road, Leavenworth, KS 66048-4946.

Prayers for the Domestic Church, Prayer for Protection in a Time of Storm or Danger, by Edward Hays, 1979. Copyright Forest of Peace Publishing, Inc., 251 Muncie Road, Leavenworth, KS 66048-4946.

Prayers for the Domestic Church, Blessed Are You, Lord Our God, Who Has Given to Each of Us a Personal Destiny and Purpose in Life, by Edward Hays, 1979. Copyright Forest of Peace Publishing, Inc., 251 Muncie Road, Leavenworth, KS 66048-4946.

Prayers for the Domestic Church, Thanksgiving Prayer upon Hearing Good News, by Edward Hays, 1979. Copyright Forest of Peace Publishing, Inc., 251 Muncie Road, Leavenworth, KS 66048-4946.

Prayers for the Domestic Church, Table Liturgy for the Feast of Thanksgiving, by Edward Hays, 1979. Copyright Forest of Peace Publishing, Inc., 251 Muncie Road, Leavenworth, KS 66048-4946.

Prayers for the Domestic Church, Mardi Gras Table Blessing, by Edward Hays, 1979. Copyright Forest of Peace Publishing, Inc., 251 Muncie Road, Leavenworth, KS 66048-4946.

St. George and the Dragon and the Quest for the Holy Grail, by Edward Hays, 1986. Copyright Forest of Peace Publishing, Inc., 251 Muncie Road, Leavenworth, KS 66048-4946.

The Secret of Staying in Love, by John Powell, S.J., 1974. Copyright Tabor Publishing, P.O. Box 7000, Allen, TX 75002-1305.

Through Seasons of the Heart, by John Powell, S.J., 1987. Copyright Tabor Publishing, P.O. Box 7000, Allen, TX 75002-1305.

The Wizard of Oz, by L. Frank Baum, with pictures by W.W. Denslow, George M. Hill Co., Chicago and New York, 1900.

PARTICIPANT QUOTES

The following are selected comments from people who have used this process.

"The greatest gift small communities have presented is personal spiritual growth. The questions and discussion of each meeting revealed the living gospel which is found in each of our personal life experiences. Because these sessions were centered in the now, the issues were much easier to understand, talk about, and discuss than sessions centered on bible study. My experience with small communities has helped me gain a deeper understanding of my faith journey, and has given me the ability to share that with others outside my group through actions and words."

"It is comforting to me to be able to belong to a group that is really listening to what I say."

"Small faith communities present a wonderful opportunity for us to be able to take time out of our busy schedules to reflect on our lives and see God in our everyday experiences."

"The small group creates, for me, a feeling of community that is much more difficult to achieve in the regular parish setting. When participating in functions with the parish those familiar faces from the small group serve to make me feel welcome, at home, a part of the whole parish."

"I am a very down to earth, concrete, 'hands on' sort of person. Basing things on real life experiences has a lot more value for me than reading from a book or the Book. It holds my attention better, and I take more home with me. Discussing personal things also builds greater trust, a tighter community."

"The combination of students, grad students and non-students is very powerful. Our orientation and life experience is so varied. As a non-student, I know I accept things from the students that I wouldn't hear from my three children who are in that same age group. Conversely, I know the students listen to me more than they would their own parents. This is so broadening for all of us. I really believe that it brings me a renewed vitality."

"Being in a small faith group has given me an opportunity to express my opinions and concerns in an atmosphere of acceptance. The small faith group has given me a group of caring friends who will support each other, exchange ideas, and this has been very enlightening."

"I am a very down to earth, concrete, 'hands on' sort of person. Basing things on real life experiences has a lot more value for me than reading from a book or The Book. It holds my attention better, and I take more home with me. Discussing personal things also builds greater trust, a tighter community."

"The combination of students, grad students and non-students is verypowerful. Our orientation and life experience is so varied. As a non-student, I know I accept things from the students that I wouldn't hear from my three children who are in that same age group. Conversely, I know the students listen to me more than they would their own parents. This is so broadening for all of us. I really believe that it brings me a renewed vitality."

"Being in a small faith group has given me an opportunity to express my opinions and concerns in an atmosphere of acceptance. The small faith group has given me a group of caring friends who will support each other, and exchange ideas and has been very enlightening."

BIBLE REFERENCES

In order of use	
1 Samuel	17:41–50
Philippians	1:6
John	4:13–14
Hebrews	6:1
2 Peter	3:18
Hebrews	10:35
Habakkuk	3:19
Ruth	1:15–17
2 Corinthians	9:6–8
Matthew	12:46–50
Mark	1:29–39
Matthew	1:18–24
Exodus	23:20–22
Exodus	17:1–3, 23:25–26, 39:42–43
Romans	8:13–17
Luke	24:13–35
Philippians	4:4–7
Mark	1:2–5, 7–8
Matthew	2:1–2, 7–11
Philippians	2:3–8
Psalm	8

In biblical order	
Exodus	17:1–3, 23:25–26, 39:42–43
Exodus	23:20–22
Ruth	1:15–17
1 Samuel	17:41–50
Psalm	8
Habakkuk	3:19
Matthew	1:18–24
Matthew	2:1–2, 7–11
Matthew	12:46–50
Mark	1:2–5, 7–8
Mark	1:29–39
Luke	24:13–35
John	4:13–14
Romans	8:13–17
2 Corinthians	9:6–8
Philippians	1:6
Philippians	2:3–8
Philippians	4:4–7
Hebrews	6:1
Hebrews	10:35
2 Peter	3:18

ABOUT THE AUTHORS

Harriet Burke, a California native and long time resident of Santa Barbara, is the mother of 5 children and is now a proud grandparent of 8. Harriet and Chuck, her very supportive husband, have been involved in parish activities and church movements for all of their married life. This includes several small groups or small community efforts, such as Marriage Encounter. Harriet has worked as a parish pastoral associate for 10 years.

William Edens, CSP, has a varied residential background after growing up in Lake Oswego, a suburb of Portland, Oregon. Bill has been active in small groups, including fraternity life and a small intentional community during graduate school days at UCLA. Bill was pastor of St. Mark's University parish during much of the time the sessions were developed. He has been an active promoter and supporter of lay leadership and small communities of faith. Bill is now pastor at St. Paul the Apostle parish in Los Angeles.

Kenneth McGuire, CSP, grew up in rural Ohio before attending graduate schools and joining the Paulists. His work in anthropology gave him an acquaintance with small group theory and their wide cultural expressions. His graduate research was with a small residential community of faith. Throughout his priestly life he has encouraged and supported the growth of small communities, one of which continues in its 21st year.

Maggie (Madelyn) Stapp and her husband, Ed, hail from the midwest but have called Santa Barbara home for the last 23 years. They have raised 5 children and are grandparents of 8. Both have been active in parish and community activities in Wisconsin and southern California, concerned with small groups and fostering lay leadership. Maggie has spent the last 10 years in a regional pastoral position for the Archdiocese of Los Angeles, working with a variety of parish groups and coordinating various conferences.

INTRODUCTION

The power of the group gatherings described in this book comes from the members of the groups *telling their stories*. Each of us, no matter who we are, has stories to tell. The only experience a person needs as a prerequisite to belonging to a Small Community of Faith (SCF) is life experience.

As we developed these group gatherings for our parish SCFs over a five-year period, we came to realize that these gatherings are applicable to all kinds of parishes, in all kinds of settings and with all kinds of people. We have discovered this, not only because the gatherings worked in our diversified parish, St. Mark's, but from the feedback received from groups throughout the United States that used this process.

This book began when the four of us, along with others from St. Mark's, attended a workshop by Father Art Baranowski. He presented a dream—how to develop small faith communities and reduce the structure of the parish. This dream pictured a parish enlivened by gatherings of people coming together to share the stories of their life and faith. We left his workshop enthused and planned to begin this process in our parish.

When we began to look for materials, we didn't find anything that seemed to fit St. Mark's. We have a parish of many cultures, backgrounds and ages. Within our boundaries one finds first generation Latino/Chicano families, a large student population including people from many cultures, a retirement community, faculty and staff from the university and families of nearby research and development industry employees.

We decided to try our hand at writing sessions for the parish, to strive to create gatherings simple enough so that all of the parishioners would feel at ease and their faith would be strengthened by their participation in a small group. The first sessions were designed to draw on the faith and life experience of each individual, no matter what their background, education, family life, previous church experience, whether 18 or 80.

The results of these gatherings surprised us. We realized that we had touched something in people that was real and energizing. Within only a few weeks we could see a change. People who had previously been strangers were greeting and visiting with one another at Sunday liturgies. People with seemingly little in common were now inquiring about a final exam, or a grandchild's surgery. When someone missed a gathering, the group realized it left a void. They called one another to accountability, to commitment for those seven weeks.

We are most grateful to the many parishioners at St. Mark's who, over the years, have participated in SCFs and given us feedback, letting us know when a session sparked or when it needed more content.

We acknowledge Father Art Baranowski for sharing his insights, experience and belief in small communities. His was the voice that activated us. Dr. Brian Hall has also earned our gratitude, personally and professionally, for his contribution to the understanding of values, from his book *The Genesis Effect*. Finally, we thank Dr. Joe and Eileen Connolly for their contribution to our understanding of effective process through many conversations and workshops.

We also have drawn on our own years of parish, community and archdiocesan experiences: Harriet Burke, pastoral associate at St. Mark's for 10 years; Bill Edens, CSP, St. Mark's pastor while much of the book was written; Kenneth McGuire, CSP, Ph.D., a former pastor at St. Mark's, and Maggie (Madelyn) Stapp, coordinator with a variety of parish ministries within the Santa Barbara Region, Archdiocese of Los Angeles.

We hope that as you begin to delve into the following pages you make the process your own. In a sense your small groups are co-creators with us. Each group brings this process to life through its own unique experiences. Our hope is that you will find the gatherings, as we did, to be a spirit-filled time of openness, prayer, reflection, dialogue and challenge to bear witness to one another. We welcome any comments or suggestions that you may have, your success stories, insights and critiques from your small groups. We continue our prayer, "Come Lord Jesus."

Advent 1995

CHAPTER 1

Process Is More Important than Content

Change is a given in our lives! Some changes are thrust upon us, some we choose and many become gradually apparent. How do we make sense of the webs of experiences, ideas and decisions in our lives? How can the church be involved in this?

At our parish, and we suspect in many parishes, Sunday mass is quite a transitory event. It's an hour or less, several people arrive late, a few leave early. Several of us see each other there every week, but even that is just a short *hello, how are you*? We often don't have a place and time to share the key happenings in our day-to-day lives, let alone our hopes and dreams for the future. Many long for a place and time to talk about these things with people who share a common faith.

The most important experiences of church are the special occasions: retreats, parish missions, special events, such as communal reconciliations, and Advent and Lenten evenings where we have the opportunity to talk about our lives and our faith. In addition, celebrations of sacraments like weddings, funerals, first communion, and the Triduum are times when we can share our faith and lives more deeply.

Since Vatican II there have been many efforts to meet the challenge of developing faith communities. The sheer size of most parishes works against easily forming a sense of community. In our daily lives in society we are valued mainly for the roles we play, not for who we are. Yet each of us needs to be valued for who we are. Jesus came that we might have life and live that life more abundantly (Jn 10:10). He came to show us that *who we are* is most important. He also showed us how to live as part of the religious institution. He lived as a faithful Jew, fulfilling the requirements of Jewish institutional laws. He also showed us how to live as a faith community. He preached to the crowds and interacted with individual persons, but primarily he formed a small group of disciples. This early group formed others. Thus the church has been a collection of small groups from its beginning.

There are many reasons, both theoretical and practical, to form small communities. There is no perfect, or even best plan. The most exciting thing is just to get started. Through our experience, we have discovered that the process of forming, the process of sharing, the process of interaction is far more important than any content. Therefore, the largest portion of this book is given to the process of group work, the way we actually do it.

As we begin, we want to share a few things about the content that we think are important, things to think about as everything proceeds. We want to look at SCFs through four different lenses: story telling, personal experience, transforming time, and values. Each is a way of getting to a deeper reality about the SCF experience.

How This Book Is Different

Others have written on the process of forming small church communities. A common theme in books about small communities is that reflection on scripture should be a major component of the time spent together. Our approach is different in that we focus on telling stories of life experience. Later on, life experiences are connected with scripture and with the church's liturgical year. We believe it is too easy to be abstract or visionary when discussing scripture. It is far more difficult to tell about our life experience. By "unpacking" life experience in a small group setting, we develop skills which are essential to discussing the meaning of scripture for our lives. With time, group members will learn to "unpack" their life experience and that of the other members and search for clues of God's presence there. We do include a reading at the beginning of each session, but contrary to the assumption on the part of many participants, the questions are not about the reading, but about our lives. The reading is a backdrop for the discussion.

We believe our significant contribution here is the *process* or the *flow* of the sessions. In the beginning, year one, fall, we focus on basic skills and values as a way of paying attention to and articulating our experience. The winter set of sessions focuses on self-care which gradually moves to intimacy and service. The spring set becomes a summary of the entire year. Telling *my* story has become telling *our* story of experiences and that is telling the Good News. In *Redemptive Intimacy*, Dick Westley reminds us that gathering and sharing our story is itself redemptive.

About the Sessions

The SCF gatherings outlined in this book are grouped according to a specific format that we have found both simple to use and helpful in promoting dialogue. Further explanation for this may be found on pp. 23–25. All sessions are numbered as follows: Year 1–2–3–4, Fall, Winter or Spring, followed by the number of the session (1–7).

You may want to revise and/or regroup our schedules somewhat to fit the specific rhythms in the life of your parish. Some sessions have more questions than it is possible to fully discuss in the allotted time. You may choose to discuss only a few questions and expand into a second session at a later time. Several groups in our parish have, in fact, found it good to repeat a specific session a few weeks later.

In this process there is an expectation of and plan for personal as well as group growth and development which may not be apparent at first. We do recommend, however, that when you schedule your group you maintain the progressive format that has been designed for the sessions.

In beginning, within the first set of sessions, people are invited to talk about general yet important facets of their lives. People come from various backgrounds and this provides an opportunity for meeting on common ground. These weeks of dialogue about personal experiences are important for building trust within the group. This is essential for continued discussion and the deepening of spiritual growth.

In the second set of sessions we recommend introducing the reading of a Sunday scripture as a closing meditation, or adding a short prayer service. The tendency is to begin immediately with a familiar form of prayer. What is familiar and good for one person may not be comfortable for another. We urge a slow patient growth with sensitivity to each person.

Experience has shown that there are rhythms to meetings which create or drain energy. Not everyone in the group will be timely in their arrival. However, if we wait until everyone arrives, others in the group will be frustrated and the meetings will run later and later. We suggest that the meetings always start on time. Anyone who arrives late can be acknowledged and encouraged to fit into the flow of the evening.

Ninety minutes are allotted from the beginning of the gathering time to the end of the wrap-up time. Another half-hour is allotted for refreshments, mixing and socializing. Therefore, the whole time from arrival to departure is two hours. Members of our groups have come to appreciate and look forward to this important two hours.

The most important task of the group facilitator is to keep the session moving through the time schedule. The temptation is to let things drag out and go overtime. The facilitator insures that the session begins and ends promptly. Within the ninety minutes some sections can be lengthened or shortened depending on the needs of the group.

Telling My Story

My story is the connective tissue of all the events, experiences and people in my life. It continually develops and even changes with various retellings. There are many episodes in each of our stories but there is only one life story. By telling and retelling we integrate, sift through, and provide coherence for all the episodes.

Groups play an important function for us. First, they are a forum to tell my story, tentative and partial at first. But as trust, acceptance and comfort build, telling the whole story becomes possible. It's also probable that we need the acceptance and encouragement of the group so that we can integrate even for ourselves some of the episodes of our own story.

The group also reinforces facets of the story. Those facets then take on more significance positively or negatively. Soon the group becomes not only the occasion to tell stories but also the source of stories; group gatherings become episodes of my story and provide the development and growth of our common group story.

The SCF serves an important function for all this. By listening to another person's story each of us becomes more aware of and able to communicate our own story and thereby discover ourselves more completely. The group dialogues help us to pay attention and to evaluate the many facets and episodes of our personal story.

Furthermore the SCF provides an important connection between "my story" and "our story": our story as parish, our story as Church, our story as Catholic People of God. The group story continues to connect to the sacred story through remembered spiritual sayings, readings, scripture and parish participation.

Transformative Time

Even more than a forum in which to tell our story, SCFs are a transformative place and *time* in our lives. All cultures perceive and speak of time in two ways; linear time and qualitative time. *The American culture deals with linear time better than with quality time.* Yet both these aspects of time have important consequences for each us and for SCFs. The linear, chronological sense of time is most significant in science, economics, social status and what we call organized society. On the other hand, quality time is most important in personal relationships, spirituality and religious rituals.

Quality time occurs when we are caught up in the moment, when we're really free and focused. Anthropologist Victor Turner calls this community time as opposed to society time. It is a side of life that emerges most fully where there are no distinctions among us in importance, status or leadership. Apart from the leader of the session, who functions as a ritual elder, all others in the group have equal status. This allows them to be guided into community. Since the leadership is rotated each session no one person is stuck with this role and no one person is allowed to lord it over the group. The skills of becoming a ritual elder are learned and shared.

Community and quality time is always experienced as special, as holy. Somehow it touches the mystery of life. When people go on a retreat they take time out of time, in a space apart: quality time and sacred space. Retreats are experienced as community which helps explain part of the excitement and fulfillment of a retreat. The most critical part is the transition to get into the retreat. Many people change their minds and avoid it at the last minute, perhaps out of fear of the holy or of relationships.

The wisdom for fullness of life is the appropriate mix of linear and quality time, of society and community. It is important that we not cling to one or resist the other. Each is necessary for different reasons. A small community of faith offers a time and place for community with quality time to happen. Faithfulness to the SCF process and time frame can help us to learn to balance these times.

The Challenge of Personal Experience

Experience is where God first encounters us since "grace builds on nature," as St. Thomas Aquinas says. We need to pay attention and learn how to recognize and communicate that experience. Much of the effectiveness of Jesus' teaching was that he addressed human experience.

In the gospel of John (Jn:12–24) Jesus is quoted as saying that unless the grain of wheat falls into the ground and dies it cannot grow, it just remains a grain of wheat. Literally it just remains alone. This metaphor functions on many levels. The institution must also die and be reborn from time to time. Groups as well as individuals need to die and be reborn many times in life. However, in actuality the seed doesn't die.

A *seed* is really *a plant packaged for shipment*. The life is stored in the seed as the embryonic living cells. This life form continues using stored food reserves in the seed. The length of time for this process depends on internal and genetic factors as well as external environmental factors. The seed can remain unchanged, from all outward appearances, for varying lengths of time. Planting the seed changes the external factors which in turn affect the internal life, and the embryonic life begins faster growth.

When the seed falls into the ground, the rigid exterior parts of it begin to change and die. Other parts of the seed are used up as food for the living embryonic cells. The essential part, the living part continues to grow. In fact, after planting the change in the environment triggers a process of growth that is so fast and dramatic that we say new life has begun. Yet, life never ceased! Part of the old life has died so that life may continue in another dramatic and visible way.

Let's spin out the metaphor for a minute. The seed coating could be the specific institutional structure of the church that changes, dies. Perhaps the Baltimore Catechism and the liturgical rules were part of that packaging of Catholic faith and life for shipment. As new life begins, parts of the prior structure die, parts are transformed and new life and faith grow and blossom. We can all provide our own stories of how the kernel of faith lived or died with the change of external circumstances. Each SCF will experience this death, by loss of members (moving, dying, etc.) and the addition of new members. Every time membership changes the group changes; in effect, it becomes a new group. In a sense the group life never ceased but is reborn.

Biblical teaching becomes a rich model, the metaphor for the monitoring, assessing and changing of our life as persons, and as church. The seed metaphor is the death-resurrection theme through which we can now see micro-parts of dying and living. These understandings, the micro-parts, can help us as we experience our own life, the micro-dyings and micro-livings, that grow to new life for us. Sometimes it seems like total death and disaster when new growth is about to begin. What parts of our present experience of life and faith must die and what parts are ready for growth?

Human growth can cease from internal or external factors; lack of food, clothing, shelter, or from personal decision because of fear or inattention as well as from environmental and social contexts. The seed that is unattended will eventually really die, unless it is cared for (stored) and planted. Just as there are many influences on the seed there are many influences on each of us personally and on us as a group. These internal and external factors, hinder or slow, encourage or aid our growth. While we cannot control these influences we can become more aware, learn to ask the right questions and modify our behavior for growth.

When our group changes through loss or addition of one or more members it is a new group—the old group has died and its passing must be mourned. If we rigidly cling to the familiar feelings and dynamics of the old group we prevent new life from entering the group.

It is of prime importance that we spend a lot of time at the beginning of a group in getting comfortable and competent in speaking about our own experiences, not just our thoughts. It is equally important to become skilled in monitoring and assessing experience to sort out our decisions concerning behaviors that produce growth.

Values Guide Us

A crucial issue in society today is: how do we transmit our values to our children, to the future generations? The disintegration of family, school and other institutions, the increase in violence, all cause us to agonize over this question. Whether conservative or liberal, it becomes apparent there must be commonly held values.

Dr. Brian Hall provides a coherent theory for organizing the values of our daily life. His insights and method underlie our whole approach to the sessions: the questions discussed, their progressive structure and the gradual development of personal and group value clarification. As our personal and group values are clarified, the values inherent in scripture are more easily discovered and connected to daily life.

Professor Brian Hall, an Episcopalian priest and research psychologist, has worked with values for over 30 years. For Hall, values are evident in behavior. *You will know them by their deeds* (Mt 7:16). Values are the priorities on which a person acts. Some values are personally chosen, some are unconsciously operating and some are the result of various social groupings within which we interact. Personal value priorities identify how we look at and respond to the world around us.

Every human value has an inner and an outer component. One example is empathy. I may have the inner image of myself as an empathetic person, but unless my outer actions bear this out I will not be perceived as empathetic. It takes a lot of skill to learn to listen in a non-judgmental way, provide cues of body language, have the art of clarifying what I hear, name feelings and affirm the person I'm listening to. Values involve behaviors and skills.

Talking, dialoguing, telling the story of our life helps us hear, and understand more fully our own internal images, our values. Hearing our story reflected back from others gives further understanding of the internal image patterns of my own life journey. Through the process of dialogue and communication, my internal images are not only identified but also can be modified. That transformation is through values. It is possible to distinguish words that are pockets of energy which identify my inner world view. These words are value words.

We all notice that some words get us excited while others tend to depress us. I am depressed by "doctor," "cloudy day" yet I get excited by "beach day" and "good reading." Values identify an experience and can link several experiences. These are the behavioral priorities which lie behind the descriptive words. As we discuss these values with others in the SCF session, that is how we identify and communicate our behavioral priorities, our values, our internal images.

A major insight from Hall's research and his subsequent theory is that he recognizes the reciprocal influence of the group and the individual. Again, we all have experienced this. For the most part values are not self-chosen but are the consequence of interaction between that which we choose and those persons and institutions with which we interact. Personal values are shaped by the group(s) within which each of us operates. Conversely personal values affect group values. This principle is often ignored to the detriment of personal and group values. SCFs are another practical way of developing personal and group Catholic values and themes in spirituality. For example, one man attended consistently an SCF for over a year in order to please his wife. During this time he could socialize afterwards, but did not talk during the group session. During the second year he began to participate. Now four years later, he is a major vocal advocate and promoter of SCFs.

Our belief is that the values belong to the group and are shared, uniquely each time, with the person. If values reside in the language as pockets of energy this makes them proper primarily to the group and secondarily to each person, even though we commonly speak and refer to "my values," and "personal values." Yet meaning and understanding are primarily the result of collective awareness, shared uniquely with each person. In the same way the virtues of faith, hope and love properly belong to the group and are shared or participated in by members of the group.

A child grows up to hold the faith and values of the parents and the cultural group(s) with which the child associates. The important question for Catholics is how the values and faith of the group, the Church, are passed on to the persons who enter as adults or as children. The RCIA (Rite of Christian Initiation of Adults) has been a revolution in recent Catholic practice. Yet it is a return to former practices. The inquirer, the seeker, is asked not only to use the mind to know the answers to questions and to be able to agree with dogmas but also to learn the style of living the gospel faith and values in the Catholic tradition. Faith expressed in action through values by certain behaviors constitutes the Catholic life, the living faith, the way of the Church.

Catholic life and faith would benefit from more concrete connections. The behaviors and stories identify the values and faith of the group and of the person. Groups of church members need to share their way of life, their values and actions with those beginning their faith-life journey. Dialogue needs to continue about the growth and development of each adult Catholic. This is what SCFs are about. This book presents a unique, experience-based, value-based method for this dialogue. We have developed a process for Catholics to talk to other Catholics about their experiences, and in the process to identify their values and virtues. These can then be compared to those from scripture and tradition. This is a very effective way to grow in wisdom, grace and age!

Clarifying Values

Hall grouped values according to skill level. Basic values like self-esteem and belonging must be mastered before we can make values requiring greater ones such as empathy operate in our life. Basic values must be practiced on a regular basis for the health and comfort of a person or group. A person usually has a variety of behaviors to do each of the values in this area. For example, the value of belonging is primarily acted out as belonging to a family. A family is not primarily a biological unit but a social unit. Interestingly there is the case where a child, twelve-year-old Amy, *divorced* her biological parents in favor of her social parents who had raised her and to whom she thought she belonged. The social family or family of nurture shares this theme more than does just a biologically connected family. Marriage is another case of change of family belonging. There are many alternative ways of belonging. I am a Boy Scout or Girl Scout, I belong to the Knights of Columbus, etc.

As we grow and change we need to discover new ways of belonging. A SCF provides a way for us to meet this basic value. Other basic values include security, personal safety/survival, belonging, self-affirmation, traditions, being liked, etc. For a healthy life each person needs to have the values in this area fulfilled adequately on a regular basis. How we do these is the focus of discussion in the early sessions. The values in this cluster are the ones that help create group bonding and a feeling of comfort and trust.

Vision or motivation values are those priorities which get us excited, those that pull us toward the future. These are what we want to become; what we want to do. Some of these values are: connection to God, intimacy, building a new church and/or world, community support, wisdom, social change for justice. This motivation area is the most tempting to spend time and energy trying to do. While these are the values that challenge us and give energy, Hall has found through his research, and we through our groups, that direct pursuit is ineffective. We need to pay just enough attention to the challenge before us that it keeps us energized, without wasting time and energy on something we are incapable of doing effectively.

It is an occupational hazard of us church folk to pay too much attention to motivation values when we don't have the skills to act them out on an ongoing, day-to-day basis. This is specifically illustrated by author Ken's personal experience. He admits he had striven for years to be a man of wisdom. This involved much reading, many workshops, endless discussions. His values profile indeed identified wisdom as a major motivational value. At the same time the profile showed detachment as the present value that was important to be developed. So for six months he concentrated on the practice of detachment and let go of some of the other wisdom pursuits. Practices for detachment, new skills development of "letting go" and being satisfied with "good enough" (the letting go of perfectionism) opened up whole new horizons. Wisdom is still the motivation value, but more practical steps are being taken.

Each of the set of sessions has a few of these motivation values for discussion and development. However, their chief effect is to keep the group energized to work for their growth values.

Growth values are where we focus our energy for skill development and practice. Anything not adequately developed in this area becomes a stumbling block for future growth, e.g., personal authority not developed can block one's ability to work for social change for justice. Important values in this area include: work, competence, health, religion, personal authority, law as rule, law as guide, service, risk, education and empathy.

Each session that we develop is based on a value. Each set of seven sessions will contain basic values (belonging, security, self-affirmation, etc.), motivational values (human dignity, building for the future, wisdom, etc.) as well as the growth values (education, health, work, etc.). When forming a group it is important to become skillful in recognizing and practicing basic values. Like the gospel story of the man who built his house on rock we need to build our lives and our groups on a strong foundation (belonging, tradition, self-esteem, caring).

By the very act of telling our story in a group, listening to one another, appreciating each other's presence, noticing when one is missing, welcoming each other with a hug, calling each other by name, remembering important events in each other's lives, spending time with each other, maintaining eye contact, we are strengthening the basic values in each other and the group.

We believe that even in the best of life and times we need to spend about twenty-five percent of our time focusing our basic values. This keeps our lives together. We also want to spend five to fifteen percent of our time looking at motivational values which challenge us, excite us and call us to the future. At least sixty to seventy percent of our time will, therefore, be spent on the practical development of the growth values. However, when there is unusually high stress in our life even more attention needs to be paid to the basics.

At the beginning of every group, and whenever new members make a change in the group membership, the basics are very important. Therefore we spend a lot of time and effort at the beginning to define, refine and put into practice the basic values. As the group develops over time, the percentage of time on each value area will revert to our recommended percentages of time. Each year will have a progression of different values. There is a list of basic values according to area in Appendix A. This list is not to be seen as exhaustive.

A SCF invites each person into a comfortable place for growth into the future. While personal growth is always individual, it also has a group component. All growth involves the work of honesty, hearing, listening and responding. The SCF provides a safe welcoming atmosphere so that each person can learn to tell their own experiences of faith, hope and love. Through this kind of interaction all of us become more fully mature Catholics. Each person's gifts, talents and dreams are noticed, supported and developed. A SCF offers a major opportunity for personal and group Catholic formation and evangelization. Members of SCFs share the role of ministry for and to themselves as well as encouraging each person to become involved in service and ministry to the entire parish. They become co-workers, co-leaders with the ordained clergy and parish staff. The vision of Vatican II is practiced where clergy and laity share in the ministry of the People of God and in the service to the world. Co-leadership training, collegiality and collaboration are the keys to the future for SCFs.

In SCFs we learn to really listen to another person, not just their words or their ideas. We begin to hear the whole person, who they really are, just as by telling and retelling my story I become more and more myself. By paying attention to the value themes the SCF reinforces the virtues of love, faith and hope in our lives, our stories. Indeed we become good news for others and others become good news for us. In reality we become the stories we tell, personally and as a group. It is through these retellings that we become co-creators with God of our story and the fulfillment of the sacred story. This is growth in grace, wisdom and age. Our personal story becomes complete at death, yet the group story continues.

CHAPTER 2

Helpful Hints for the Process

Methodology

When, where and how to meet are primary questions for every beginning. Each group will eventually develop its own rhythm in these areas. Yet we live in modern American society which will always have an effect. Therefore we have chosen, up front, to take that cultural rhythm into account.

For most of us, the period from Thanksgiving to New Year's, is a very busy time. Similarly Holy Week and Easter plus some time on either or both sides is a busy time. The period at the end of the school year beginning in May through June is another busy time. Summer is traditionally a time for summer camps, vacation, and travel. Therefore, we have divided the year into three sets of seven sessions each. These sets can fit well into the American time rhythm: from mid-September to Thanksgiving, again from January-February into March, and in most years post Easter into May. These three calendar times offer the best *windows for success* for group beginnings.

We suggest meeting weekly during these three blocks of time. Persons and agendas get easily lost, especially at the beginning. The seven sessions are not over-burdensome for the short term, and if for some reason a group needs to skip a week the schedule can slip and still fit into the cultural rhythm. The group also may want to add a session for a social or celebration together to fit the seasonal occasion. In fact, most of our parish groups add an evening for a dinner social at the end of each set of gatherings. Sometimes they may take on a common project for a day or evening. Each group can work out its specific schedule. The whole point is to meet enough to do the spiritual work and avoid so many meetings that people get burned out. Every parish or group can modify and adapt these sessions to their own best schedules.

We also suggest that a group begin with people from differing generations and if possible more than one of each. From our experience, in order for good dialogue to develop, groups should not be less than seven or more than fifteen.

Groups will need to develop cohesion. Yet just as personal needs change so do group needs change. We suggest at least every two to three years that every group should experience some change. This will probably happen in the normal course of group life. In American culture there is so much movement that this probably will happen without planning it. However, a group that has successfully been together for two or three years would do well to split itself in half, welcome new members and therefore contribute to spreading the enthusiasm and process. By whatever means the membership change happens, it will involve more and more people so that more people will experience the personal change and growth that takes place. All this will aid change and growth in the whole church and the world.

In the past, we have added new people to existing groups—groups that have been in existence for two or more years. A note of caution to the existing group: do not assume that the new members can jump right in and be at the same level of sharing skills, familiarity with the process or the members of the group. The experienced members may perceive that the new members fit in well and seem at ease in the sessions. This may be a problem of discernment for the group, because the new members are probably being carried by the group and do not have the same depth of understanding or experience in the process. We do not advise having new members create sessions for the group before being seasoned in the method.

The other half of the note of caution is that the new members will more than likely change the dynamics of the group. Experienced members may note a change in attitude about their trust level and ability to risk in sharing. One suggestion we have to overcome this dual problem is to go back to year one fall, winter, or spring and repeat a few of the beginning sessions. All of these focus on connections, welcome and hospitality. The sharing questions are at a "getting to know you" level. They also have emphasis on the ground rules for sharing and confidentiality.

A common danger in developing a personal interior life is to become self-absorbed. In the same way, as a group develops its particular group identity and life together, the temptation and danger is for too great a focus within the group. There are plenty of examples, e.g., Jonestown and the Branch Davidians. Some outward focus is always necessary. In fact, the whole point, personally as well as for the group, is to focus outward on the world of God's creation and our responsible participation in it. Small group participation *and* outward focus facilitate both personal and group growth and development.

We have all been part of groups that consistently begin late or run way over the stated closing time. From experience we strongly encourage following the session format provided, especially in the beginning. Starting the session on time, whether there are three or thirteen people present, sets an example for the future. As people grow to enjoy the dialogue and sharing, from our experience, they will make every effort to arrive promptly.

With guidance from the group facilitator every session is designed to last no longer than 90 minutes. Another half-hour is set aside for refreshments and socializing. The whole process does not exceed two hours. People have expressed appreciation for this respecting of their time.

The group facilitator's primary role is to keep the session moving while being sensitive to the specific needs of the group. Within the session, he/she may adjust the schedule. At times, more time may be needed in the small or large groups. However, when something is expanded, then something else needs to be curtailed. As a rule it is better to leave people "thirsting for more" than letting the discussion drag out. As the last words are said people begin to lose interest and boredom quickly is evident.

Experience Is the First and the Best Teacher

This is perhaps the key to our method as contrasted to other approaches. A major premise of this book is that the Spirit of God speaks to each one of us through our experiences. We continually discover more of God's plan for us and for all creation. Therefore, learning to pay attention to the fullness of personal experience enhances the Spirit's call to us personally and as People of God. Articulating my experience and seeing and hearing other people's response aids me in interpreting my own personal experience. We do this all the time, yet most of the time inadvertently, unintentionally and ambiguously.

Personal lives consist of particular events, people, things. Personal memories, hopes and goals are specific for everyone. We do not all share the same great ideals. In small groups people learn to listen to the nitty-gritty of life, the uniqueness of one's own life as well as the specialness of others' lives. Life can easily become fragmented as we are pulled in many directions. The SCF offers a place to bring it all together.

Several people have been uneasy at the beginning when someone begins to tell the more private aspects of their life story. But later they feel privileged to know them on a much deeper level. One group member said, *"It was very difficult for me at first to talk about myself, about my life, other than the general descriptions of myself. I guess I paid very little attention to specific events and sometimes even people. I know I analyzed a lot. I was always trying to figure out reasons why. Finally, listening to other people talk about specific parts of their lives, I found myself paying real attention to the events of my own life."*

SCFs can provide for parishes a real and necessary means for people to share and integrate their lives. Some will fear that their individuality will be smothered. However, we are convinced that strong persons make strong communities, just as strong communities make for strong persons. The inverse, of course, is also true. Weak people make weak communities; weak communities attract weak people. The fullness of community is difficult to reach. This takes lots of time, practice and patience. Skills of listening, responding, focusing and following the dialogue are necessary. Each person needs to make time management decisions to be present and to focus on being present.

Our experience has consistently shown the biggest problem is to *get out of our heads* and into contact with our emotions and into fuller contact with the lives of others. Understanding is important, yet experience and feelings are prior to understanding. The emphasis in this book is on experience, experience, experience.

The process of sharing experience, talking specifically, and personally, along with active listening are basic for SCFs to continue for any significant length of time. We have found that one of the easiest, yet hardest, things is to get people talking about themselves. Self-disclosure requires skills that we all have to some degree but in every case they can be improved. The self-talk invariably begins in the head with *"my ideas"* or *"I think."* Some of us proceed faster than others to speaking of emotions: sorrows, joys, hopes, dreams. Continued practice and trust are important as we progress to holistic dialogue and to the grasping of God's revelation for us.

Our experience, our sharing, our discussion/dialogues are always within the context of scripture and tradition, for that is who we are even if not directly mentioned. There is certainly the temptation to find out what scripture says or what tradition means, first. Then we can apply it to our lives. In reality our life experiences are the primary material of our spiritual lives. God deals with us, challenges us, heals us, forgives us, calls us through our experiences. After we recognize and reflect on them, we can use scripture and tradition to confirm God's work with us.

Some people may think that we shortchange the use of scripture within the groups. On the contrary we believe that scripture can keep us distracted from the real rich agenda of faith and life. The primary agenda of life and therefore our faith is our daily life. Paying attention to what is happening, not shutting out parts or paying attention to only what we expect or want is very important. The second agenda of life and faith is assessing the meaning of life's experiences, and this is where scripture and tradition are important. Therefore, the first task of our faith community, large and small, is to help us pay attention to all the details of daily life. Small groups can help us avoid rose-colored glasses as well as dull gray tints. Therefore during the first year we suggest some short reading at the beginning of each session to focus attention for the time. We do suggest a variety of readings here; fairy tales, spiritual authors, scripture.

However, from our personal experiences as well as our pastoral ministry experience we have become convinced that sufficient reflection on personal experience is often lacking. Most of us lack the skills to pay attention, to notice and assess the various facets of our experience. Furthermore, there is a popular piety that shuns this worldly experience and tries to focus on Jesus and scriptural passages almost exclusively.

Three theological convictions support our work. 1) Awareness is the first movement and requirement of the spiritual life. 2) The Holy Spirit comes through our experiences. 3) Scripture and tradition are the recorded experiences of the People of God in the past.

Our experience reveals that people are on a broad spectrum in their spiritual journey. But two major groups stand out and need our attention. First, many people leading very ordinary, good lives personally feel they are not worthy or are not holy enough to really get involved in the church. Many of these are convinced that a radical change of life would be necessary before they could really be involved and they therefore shy away. The second group of people have developed a personally meaningful spiritual routine which works for them, but really sets them apart from others. It almost becomes, although not intended as such, an elitist attitude. The scriptural story of the Pharisee and the tax collector is a caricature of these two groups.

We have designed the method or process for this book so that all people will mutually benefit. The book spends the first year's sessions focusing almost solely on various facets of experiences and basic values so that everyone may share insights and learn to see, feel, and hear more fully. Therefore everyone can profit from the riches of the personal as well as group reflections.

Furthermore, it is our belief that after a session focused on some special aspect of experience a person hears scripture from a different angle. The reading from the church's spiritual tradition or scripture will take on added meaning because we will hear it from the various points of view of where we are when it is read: joyful, sad, expectant. So rather than focus on the critical textual meaning, we just let it be and continue the major focus on life experiences. In later sessions, years three and four, the focus on experience, scripture and tradition becomes integrated.

Some of the groups that have tried this method were anxious to rush on to scripture at the beginning. However, as they stayed with the process, becoming comfortable and adept at noticing and assessing their experience, the relationship to scripture began to flow naturally. Those who are currently in the third and fourth year have a rich repertoire of experience, tradition and scripture for the faith dialogue. During the second set of sessions we suggest that each session close with a reading from scripture, preferably the readings for the Sunday to come, or possibly a reading from the church's spiritual tradition. We don't recommend that this be discussed, just absorbed. During the third and fourth years the themes for each session closely follow the liturgical year and reflection on the appropriate scripture reading for these feasts.

The personal experience of the people of each group forms the content of this book. Our significant contribution is the process by which this is developed. There will be a short reading, teaching, or scripture quote near the beginning of each session. The point of this is not to *study* or *understand*. The reading, scripture, or teaching in some way relates to the focus questions for that session. But the questions for each session which evoke the experience of every person are the point for reflection and dialogue. The main focus of each session is the personal reflection and response to the questions concerning the session's topic.

During the second series of sessions we recommend that the group end its session by listening to someone read the scripture for the following Sunday. Following the personal dialogues about experiences and values, the scripture will be heard differently. Also during the following week they will take on more significance as well as when the scriptures are read at mass on Sunday. Later on in the process we end sessions by alternating the reading of scripture with short inspirational readings from tradition.

The questions for each session in every case deal with whatever response they arouse in the hearers. The major part of the evening is spent recognizing whatever responses are within, then learning to put those into words and to speak them. Of equal importance, is to listen, hear others' responses to the original question as well as their response to my words. Reciprocally being able to really listen to the words and response of another, is important. This can be done verbally or non-verbally. It is important to validate one another and to let the speaker know he/she has been heard. This is what we call *active listening*.

The process we practice and which we recommend is *structured personal dialogue*. Discussion connotes concentration on thinking and ideas. For us, dialogue focuses more on the entire content; body language, emotional aspects, spiritual connections and groundings, as well as thoughts and ideas. The whole person is involved in the dialogue.

All dialogue is helpful. However, a structured approach permits the dialogue to lay good foundations for personal and group development. The structure permits everyone to feel comfortable and to participate by providing freedom and protection for more intimate dialogue. It includes energizing parts, yet does not allow that hopeful, *wanna-be* part of ourselves to become dominant and hamper the most important part of personal learning and skill development.

We truly believe that when two or three are gathered in Christ's name the Spirit is there. Therefore the focus is on learning to listen to the Spirit *within and among us*. This is the primary learning point. While learning more about scripture, tradition and theology is important, it is secondary. The voice of the Spirit though our experiences grounds us in God, and the Spirit will always call us into deeper study and learning as well as deeper involvement in the world around us for social care, freedom and justice.

The more we are aware of our experiences, the places, the circumstances, and the people, then we can begin to better understand God's word within our lives as well. The story of Samuel and Eli is an example of this (see 1 Sam 3:1–18). Young Samuel heard a voice and thought that Eli had called him. He went and asked Eli what he wanted. Eli had not called and told Samuel to go back to sleep. Finally Eli thought this might be God calling Samuel so he suggested how Samuel could test it and find out. Samuel's answer did not come from authority, tradition or scripture. Only after several experiences were shared did it become clear what might be happening, and then the voice of God in his experience could be heard.

The biblical story of Samuel illustrates another American propensity. We are often tempted to view experience as a one-time thing. Just do it and get it over with. *Been there, done that*. Yet real life experiences are often repeated. Rather than being boring maybe there's more to be gained. The call of God's Spirit becomes clearer and clearer through repeated experiences and the telling and retelling of them. Therefore, through sharing stories we can replace boredom with excitement. We each tend to construct our own version of life from personal experience. Yet shared experiences create deeper, richer lives. Only through deep personal sharing within a group do we become truly ourselves, in touch with our soul, our deepest self. The exciting thing is that through deeper and deeper personal sharing with another or others, we develop into soul mates. This transformation thrives within communities of faith; friendship and partnership wither in isolation. This certainly also applies to marriage partners.

The first responsibility of SCFs is to connect persons of faith. The process of their connections, sharings, and the bonds developed sharpen the skills of self-perception and self-reflection. Therefore self-discovery is enhanced at the same time that discovery of the other happens. Within a community of faith, while all this is happening a deeper experience and discovery of God is taking place.

Through the small group process of skill development, each person improves the quality of her/his own experiences by focusing attention and energy. The group interaction helps each person to recognize his/her own complexity and, therefore, to act more effectively in the complex world. In addition to the personal discovery that has been taking place, each person has been continually developing personal and social skills which are useful throughout the many other areas of life.

Learned Wisdom

When a group first forms, or later when a new person joins the group, there will often be a concern for *more* content. What does this or that mean? The question indicates a desire for more information, more knowledge, more ideas to fulfill a primary urge for understanding. This is the continuation of a long developed habit in our culture, which has its place and has served us well. However, SCFs deal with the whole person, not just the mind and understanding. Concern for more content may serve as a means of avoiding nonrational elements: emotions, presence, spirit and therefore dealing with the whole range of being a person. It is always easier to deal only with that which is familiar. The process for SCFs is the transformation or *metanoia* of life and faith. St. Paul says *there are in the end three things that are important: faith, hope and love.* These things are known by the way we live. By becoming aware of the way, the schedule, rhythm, methodology, process of our lives we discover more fully, self, others, God. Therefore the process, the way we live is the core of the Small Community of Faith experience.

SCFs often become a family of choice. This time around we have the chance to do it right (at least better) as each person is not limited to past assigned family roles. The group is a primary learning place, especially for developing interpersonal (social) skills. There is a lot of reciprocal mentoring that develops. No one is alone on the journey of life and everyone can share insights of experience by foresight or hindsight. These communities of faith share life and are support groups, not education or study groups.

From this point of view the intergenerational composition is most significant. Often in our groups a young adult will say, *"It is so important to be able to talk with someone the age of my parents. Now I can understand them better."* Also the older group members will comment about *"how great it is to really talk to young people and begin to share their excitement and feel myself important again."* The depth of sharing and relating will vary from person to person, but will aid each in coming to know themselves more clearly and to recognize their faith journey. The persons in the group will soon begin to want to enjoy celebrating life together. Often the whole group will attend a graduation, a wedding, a Lenten series, or a funeral. The intergenerational aspect enriches the perspective of the young and the old by making present a longer line of experiences. It also supports equal footing for all across age and experience differences.

Dos and Don'ts for Success

1) **Keep a connection with the local parish.** An appointed group leader may be counterproductive. We have found that, similar to 12-Step programs, people appreciate an egalitarian process of shared responsibility and accountability. However there does need to be a liaison person in every group who can remain constant for a longer period, e.g., a year. This person coordinates with the parish staff and with other groups. Going off on your own as a group is ultimately unhealthy and dangerous for faith development. Those groups who stay connected, form and reform the church. Those who isolate might possibly become cults or heresies. God's revelation from the beginning has come to a community, to God's people. Individual persons are involved but never alone.

2) **Each group needs to keep a mixture of ages, sexes, and interests.** This facilitates focusing on *being* and the broad, yet specific experiences of life. Avoid special interest groups which reinforce each other to keep focusing on the doing of their interest rather than sharing their journey of life and faith. (Interest groups are good but do not make faith sharing groups.)

3) **Meetings need to be frequent, usually once per week.** The process for relationship development and bonding to take place needs frequent contact, at least in the first stages. Later on, meetings may be less frequent, maybe every other week and in some cases monthly.

4) **There needs to be significant interaction through body language and spoken words.** The rules or covenant for the meetings need to be carefully worked out to do these things. To fully participate people have to be present, to share personal experiences, to join in common prayer, and reading.

5) **Focus on the process and away from content.** We Americans are cerebral enough and need more skills and practice in affective interaction. Affect more than intellect creates bonds between persons.

6) **Each person needs to express ideas and feelings, each at an appropriate level.** Every person's sharing will vary yet deepen with time. No one reveals more than they deem appropriate and the group itself becomes the support for such personal decisions.

7) **If problems arise these should be discussed openly, truthfully without rushing to a solution, or only part of the group doing the discussing.** Often the better action is to *live with the problem* for a while as a group, after it has been openly acknowledged. During that time significant things can happen that transform and give insight.

8) **Share personal special needs, hopes and problems.** That will help others to understand personal moods and needs and offer support.

9) **People need to be mutually accountable to each other, not just to a leader.** All are responsible and accountable. This is important as part of each person's growth in responsibility and accountability. The responsibilities are easily rotated, from hosting to facilitation. We have found that it is good to rotate the facilitator for the gatherings with each person taking a turn. This develops shared authority and responsibility and avoids mini-pastors.

10) **Begin to treasure one's self and honor others,** by listening, appreciating and touching as appropriate. Learning to say *I appreciate that* or *I appreciate you* is new for many people. The need and ability to touch varies also.

11) **Continuity and change are both needed.** Too much of either is detrimental. After a group gets going the bonding becomes so strong and the people feel so comfortable and supported they do not want to change. On one hand this is good and on the other this is the first step toward developing elitism and exclusivity. Also it gives a false sense of, "This is the only group for me." It deprives the members of the group and others of talking about and *sharing the good news.*

12) **A parish needs to develop a network of small communities of faith.** There needs to be some interchangeability so that newcomers are always welcome and that they are not the only new persons. Each person can take the skills and faith developed in this group and integrate into another or start another group. We suggest that a group go no more than three years without some membership change. Also, each person should experience a change every four to five years.

13) **Avoid a hypercritical spirit or negative attitude.** This is very easy to slip into personally and as a group. Negatives should be noted just as differences are noted. But the common and the positive are so much more plentiful. Negativism is usually an indicator of something deeper, such as unresolved anger or unadmitted conflict. It also may be the result of habit. Current U.S. culture heavily accents the negative, the critical. For the long haul, groups last if they are not dragged down by the negative. Groups that create positive energy and excitement last.

14) **Elitism is always a temptation.** *Our group is the best* or *we all showed up* are among many indicators. An attitude that this is so good for me and us that everybody should do it can develop. There are many paths to elitism.

15) **Avoid fascination with the marvelous and the extraordinary** which is a deep human temptation. God works in the ordinary of our lives. The usual advice of spiritual directors is *if you have the choice between an ordinary and extraordinary action, choose the ordinary.* A major temptation is to see oneself as extraordinary or different from others. God provides in our life what is needed and necessary. Seeking special penances or special prayers should be avoided.

16) **The small community of faith is a support group concerned primarily with being.** Be cautious of letting it become an education group although education will happen. Avoid letting it become a social action group, although each person should be moved to some form of action for social care (care for the poor) or social justice (working for change in social roles or rules). Each person's faith should be seen in action. The group as a whole may do an action for education, or social justice but this should not be a regular part of the group's time together.

17) **Social justice actions as a group should be limited.** There will be a strong temptation to do *good works* together. Because of the regular transformations, learnings and support within the group each person will want to get involved in doing something to make a better world. Each person's best choice will be what appeals to them. A common project will be less appealing and less effective. Each person should be encouraged to go where they feel challenged and called. The group will continue as a support-base for members' projects. A very occasional specific group project would be fine.

18) **Socializing with members of the group** is good and important. However, each person's social life needs to spread beyond group members. Exclusive personal social contact within the group is the first step to exclusiveness.

Mutual Accountabilities—Parish and SCFs

Accountabilities of group members:
    participating in parish worship
    serving in ministries for parish
    committing to help out for community service
    avoiding cliquishness
    accepting change in my group gracefully
        allowing members to leave
        welcoming new members
    promoting a hospitable atmosphere in the parish
    attending to my personal spiritual growth
    talking up small communities with other parishioners
    taking my share of responsibility for the life of the
        group and the parish

taking my turn at facilitation, hosting, etc.
committing myself to really listening to other group members

Accountabilities of the pastoral staff:
articulating a new vision of church
as community—groups are church
coordinating the formation of groups
providing materials for use in groups
meeting with group liaisons
promoting positive images in the parish concerning
small communities of faith
inviting parishioners to recognize the communities
that already exist
forming a network of SFCs for mutual enrichment
and nourishment
coordinating parish-wide large-group gatherings
of SCFs on quarterly, yearly basis
offering educational and formational opportunities
collaborating with the diocese and bishop
collaborating with other parishes

Just as words without action are hollow, so too, involvement in a small community of faith will become faithless unless each person puts that faith into action through parish and institutional channels for a Christ-centered life.

CHAPTER 3

Guidelines and Special Sessions

Getting Started

This is where the rubber hits the road. Now that we have some group theory, it's time to get started forming these groups in our parish. This chapter contains diverse exercises, guidelines and sessions that we have found useful. Several are referenced in the text for regular use in SCF meetings. Many others are suggested sessions for gatherings for all the parish groups as well as for deanery and regional gatherings of groups. These larger gatherings help avoid isolation and small group elitism. There is also a larger dynamic at work. SCF members experience a real belonging to the larger church, parish, region, diocese and world church. This is your start-up kit.

Group Leadership

Leadership comes in various styles. Servant-leadership is a concept made popular by Robert Greenleaf in the 1970s and rediscovered in the 1990s. (1) Greenleaf says that the test of servant-leadership is to ask the question: "Do those being served grow stronger, freer, more autonomous, more likely themselves to become servant leaders?" (2) If the leadership in the group is truly servant-leadership, the members of the group should be growing in the ability to be servant leaders through role-modeling and through some opportunity to practice.

One of the goals of this process is to enrich the church by training servant leaders. We think it is very important that any leadership in the groups be *shared* leadership; that group leadership be a collaborative effort, rather than having one pastoral facilitator of the group who is seen as an extension of the pastor of the parish. In our groups we suggest that the leadership be rotated at least once every several weeks or meetings. We found that many groups soon began regular rotations weekly. Further, at each meeting, everyone in the group is encouraged to see themselves as a co-leader, taking responsibility for the success of the group.

Each group should also have a *contact* or *liaison* person who is constant for the year.

This provides a way for information to flow from the group to the parish staff and from the staff to the group. It is still important that every person in the group to be co-responsible for making connection with the parish, the region and the diocese. Each person should be conscious of making connections with other groups and with the larger church.

An Introductory Evening for Parish Small Community of Faith

7:30 Hospitality

(greeters' name tags, marking pens, sheets of questions for discussion, coffee, tea, creamer, sugar, punch and cookies needed)

7:35 Welcome

MC (master of ceremonies) or MCs for the evening should handle this section and make the following points. We find it is beneficial to have a male and female.

—this is an informational evening about SCFs.

—the best way to understand how they work and what they are about is to experience a group.

—tonight we will form mini groups of 4–6 and afterward we will come back and talk about the formation and have time for questions.

MC will ask for the following actions during the evening.

—we will break into small groups.

—count off around the room (calculate how many groups you need according to the number of people you have. (Groups of 4–6 are best.)

—announce where each group should meet. (If possible have chairs set up in circles for these groups, if not everyone carry one chair.)

—announce the evening's facilitator for each group.

7:40 Have people move and get settled into groups

The facilitators in each group will ask everyone to introduce themselves. Then they should read the Guidelines for Sharing (pp. 30–31) (you may want to make copies available to hand to everyone).

7:45 Ask someone to lead a focus exercise. Choose one from pp. 31–33.

—a minute of silence afterward is good.

Reading:

A woman dreamed she walked into a brand-new marketplace and, to her surprise, found God behind the counter. "What do you sell here?" she asked. "Everything your heart desires," said God. Hardly daring to believe what she was hearing, the woman decided to ask for the best things a human being could wish for. "I want peace of mind and love and happiness and wisdom and freedom from fear," she said. Then as an after-thought, she added, "not just for me, for everyone on earth." God smiled, "I think you've got me wrong, my dear," He said, "We don't sell fruits here, only seeds."

from Taking Flight by Anthony de Mello, S.J., p. 103

Facilitator: Pause for 1–2 minutes after the reading for reflection. Then ask your group of 5–6 to further divide into groups of 2–3. Pass out sheets of questions and ask people to read the cluster of questions for each number, pausing a minute to reflect and then discussing them before moving on to the next cluster of questions.

Questions: (these can be prepared beforehand for passing out)

1. People often plant seeds in our lives.
   Who are some of your "seed planters"?
   (people in your family, education, workplace, etc.)

2. In talking about family seeds planted, did this cause you to identify or reflect on your roots?
   When did your family/ancestry come to the U.S.?
   What is a favorite ethnic food or tradition in your family?

3. When did you first come to the parish?
   What helped you feel "rooted" here?

8:10 Have the groups of 2–3 reassemble to their original small groups.
   Talk about what you heard or identified with in the groups.

8:20 Have all the small groups form one large group for teaching.

8:22 Pastor or staff person
   Talk about purposes of small groups SCFs.
   Make spiritual connection.
   Give some vision for the parish groups.

8:30 Another staff person (preferably always a male/female modeling)
   Talk about how the SCF process takes place in our parish. Mention that each meeting has a theme and that the discussion/dialogue questions are based on life experiences. We believe that God is in all things, so all experiences are revelations. We meet in homes and each member of the group has a chance to host, a chance to facilitate, a chance to bring refreshments. Mention how important it is to have a mixture of different people and how important it is to keep to the time frame (7:00 to 8:30 for talking and 8:30 to 9:00 for refreshments and socializing within a 7–8 week time frame).

8:35 MCs:
   Questions from the large group

8:42 MCs:

We invite you to sign up (have a way for this to be done).

Stay around and talk with others.

Connect with others you would like to be in a group with.

Someone will call you to set up the first group meeting.

Invite everyone to stay for dessert and conversation.

Thanks to all for coming.

8:45 Closing Prayer

8:50 Refreshments

Forming Your Own Groups

When the information evening is over, it is the task of someone in the parish to divide the people into groups. (Someone from the staff should be involved.) If you have existing groups, and they have room, the easy solution is to add the new people to those groups. If you are just beginning and need to form all new groups, we have a few suggestions for startup.

If at all possible, it is good to have an intergenerational mix. We have found that there are many kinds of wisdom to be shared across generations. To put all young people together or all the elderly together is to short-circuit sharing that wisdom. The same is true of gender and race mix. Make the groups as diverse as possible, although try not to isolate a person as the *only* one (e.g., African-American, young, Asian) in the group. Another note of caution: do not begin a group with people who are all new to the parish. They need someone to help make connections. Ideally, only two or three new members should be in various groups for adequate integration into the parish.

As you are breaking the list into groups you will probably notice that some persons you know possess the qualities for running a meeting, keeping time, and being hospitable. These are the people you will want to ask to facilitate the first two or three meetings of the group. They should also be good at encouraging others into co-leadership, so that others have positive experiences in leadership and gain confidence.

Overview of Sessions

1) **Gathering and welcoming** is first on the agenda, and is very important. The facilitator's main concern is to get everyone greeted and see that they feel comfortable. Later on, this is easier and everyone will enter into making sure this happens.

   This part extends from the facilitator gathering people, announcing the theme and ends with asking for people to do readings, etc. It also includes time for informal sharing by each person about how their week has gone. This is an important aspect of the evening. It helps to know what is happening in people's day-to-day lives.

2) **Focus Exercise** is a time to help people relax and to be present for whatever happens in the session. There are suggested exercises and others may be used. Keep this section brief.

> **A note:** We have not included this in the first couple of sessions as it is important to get people acquainted and used to talking. Some people will have done something like this before, but it may be new to others. So we suggest that it be done after 2–3 meetings. Then it becomes a regular part of the session.

3) **Reflective Reading** is done to help concentrate on the theme for the evening. It is primarily for listening and absorbing, not for discussion and learning. Many of us immediately want to focus on what it said and what it means, which takes the focus off the main purpose of the session, which is talking about personal experiences. The readings do relate to the theme but are not meant to distract from personal experiences of the theme, which is the center of the dialogue.

4) **Small Group Discussions** are meant to give everyone a chance to speak rather than have to take turns in a large group. More can be said by more people in a shorter time. Also some people are more comfortable, initially, sharing in small groups.

5) **Large Group Discussions** are a means of drawing out some of the themes or similarities talked about in the small groups.

> **A note:** The small group, large group discussions can be reversed, or at times other variations can take place.

6) **Wrap-up and Evaluation** are a means of winding down and reviewing the session. This is the time to get ready for the next meeting and plan all the details.

7) **Closing Options** are not used in the first set of sessions so that people can get used to the general flow. Beginning in the second set of sessions we suggest some form of formal closing, reading from scripture being the most universally favored, or a reading from our spiritual tradition or a form of prayer. Each group will develop its own style. At the beginning care should be taken to see that everyone is comfortable—there are many differing prayer styles currently used. Some people would like to say a decade of the rosary, others want time for spontaneous prayer, still others a time of quiet contemplation.

8) **Refreshments** are important at the end to help people mingle and talk further about themselves in a very informal way. We use refreshments rather than desserts for good reason—each group will have its preferences. This time should be kept brief with the half hour schedule. The temptation is to let it drag on. People appreciate being able to leave in good grace on time.

Prayer

You will notice that in the first group of sessions, we don't have any prayer suggestions. This is done intentionally. Many people who first try a small community of faith are afraid that they are getting into something that is far too "religious" for them. It is enough that they get to know the other people in the group, test out the ways of talking about the issues and their story. Gradually they will begin to feel comfortable with themselves as a part of the group. If they first came into a group and the prayer was deep and meditative, or very verbally expressive, and this was not their style, they could be very put off. We have also experienced non-Catholic spouses coming to the group who are not too sure about this "Catholic" thing. From the input we have received, it seems that it is better to give some time at the beginning for people to get acquainted with this "new way" and with each other. As the sessions progress we have added prayer suggestions for closing. Each group is different and will respond to prayer in a variety of ways. It is important to be sensitive to that and ask the members to give their suggestions and preferences. The prayers we have given are merely suggestions. We think it is far better to have people in the group create their own. As the group grows together its prayer will grow and change. Therefore it is important to take these steps slowly and patiently. Each person will have to be respectful of all the others, so that the working out of common prayer is not coercive in any way. But what better way to get to know each other in a more personal way than to hear the way we each pray!

As the group continues to meet, we suggest that different people be responsible for the prayer of the evening. This is particularly meaningful at the end of a series, where a special theme can be celebrated. We have added prayers also because people have said that they simply don't have time to do extra planning. As time goes on it is important to develop this skill, so that people within the group can do the planning not only of the prayer, but of the evenings. In our bibliography we have listed several books that are good resources for prayer experiences. Feel free to use them, change them, and add to them. It is always a good way to end the meeting. This ending could also use one of the readings for the upcoming Sunday mass.

Examples for Closing Prayers

Closing Prayer #1

In the beginning, Lord God,
    You alone existed: eternally one
    yet pregnant in the fullness of unity.
Full to overflowing,
    You, Father of All Life, exploded outward
    in a billion bits and pieces.

Your Words became flesh,
      whirling in shining stars, shimmering suns
      and in genesis glimmering galaxies.
You, my God, spoke,
      and Your Words became flesh:
      in sun and moon, earth and seas,
      mountains and gentle hills,
      rolling rivers and silent streams.
You, my God, spoke,
      and Your Words became flesh:
      in winged bird, in deer and elephant,
      in grazing cow, racing horse and fish of the deep.
Your Words, so unique and so varied,
      filled the earth also with rabbit, squirrel and ant.
And all Your Words were beautiful,
      and all were good. Amen
                    edited from *Prayers for the Domestic Church* by Edward Hays, p. 53

Closing Prayer #2

W. We thank You, God of Mysterious Ways,
      that You have a holy design for each of us.

   We rejoice that we are, each of us, special to You,
      that our names are written in the palm of Your hand
      and our place in history, our purpose for existing,
      is known within Your heart, since endless ages.

M. We are grateful for that long line of holy people,
      who since ancient times have inspired others
      by their faithfulness to their own special destinies.

   They, by their very lives, shout out to us
      not to compromise our destinies,
      but to live fully within Your eternal design.

All: Blessed are You, Inscrutable Lord,
      for those events, persons, talents and loves
      which have helped us to discover
   adventure and purpose, fruitfulness and meaning,
      in our sometimes empty
   and seemingly insignificant lives.
   Blessed are You
      for teachers, parents and other guides

who call us out
    from the cocoon of comfort and contentment
    to embark upon that unique path
    which You have set forth
    for each of Your sons and daughters.
Blessed are You, Lord our God,
    who has given to each of us
    a personal destiny and purpose in life.
        AMEN.

edited from Prayers for the Domestic Church by Edward Hays, p. 59

Closing Prayer #3

I   O God, how precious it is for us
       And how pleasing it must be to You
    When Your daughters and sons learn how to live and
       work together in unity!

II   It is in the measure that we do this
       that we begin to resemble You
    And to carry out most effectively Your purposes
       in our disjointed and discordant world.

I   Come, let us together bless God's name,
       rejoice in Your loving concern for us,
       declare Your worth to all creatures,
       and walk in obedience to God's will.

II   It is the same God who made heaven and earth
       and all of us who dwell therein
    Let us worship and serve God together.

ALL: "That they may be one, Lord, as you are in me and I in you; that they all may be one in us." For this do we pray, Lord, that the hope and the prayer of Jesus may be fulfilled in us this day as we live together, work together, take risks together, suffer together, and rejoice together. Come, Lord, send Your Spirit into us to make us one in You and in all.

from "Good Lord, Where Are You?" by Leslie Brandt
in Let's Pray 2! by Br. Charles Reutemann, F.S.C., p. 36

Closing Prayer #4

My Lord and my God,
    such good news has come today,
    and I am overjoyed with its bright message.
My heart is full to overflowing with gratitude to You

who are the source of all good things.
Like a child, joy fills the whole of me,
    each cell is celebrating,
    each muscle is alive with delight.
My prayer has been that in all things
    I might do Your holy will,
    in the great as well as small events of my life.
I lift up my heart in thanksgiving
    that this blessing, by Your design,
    is to be part of my life-journey.
May I use this great blessing
    to bring me closer to You, my God,
    and the world closer to peace.

Lord, I ask that this flame of joy ever illuminate my life
    and be a lamp unto my prayers. AMEN

edited from *Prayers for the Domestic Church* by Edward Hays, p. 41

Guidelines for Sharing

Ground Rules for Speaking

Speak out of one's own truth and experience.

Respect the contributions of others.

What is shared remains in the room—respect confidentiality.

Be sure to refer back to the questions to remain focused—
    don't get sidetracked.

Be an active listener. Try to sense another's feelings and experiences.
    Take the risk of being changed.

Avoid a judgmental attitude.

Helpful Hints for Listening

Keep eye contact with the person speaking.

Let the other person complete a thought; don't jump in with your comment.

Ask a question if you don't understand what a person said.

Give some form of feedback to let the person know you hear.

Helpful Hints for Being a Full Participant in the Group

Indicate affirmation of each person.

    This does not mean agreement with what everyone says.

Demonstrate trust, help group members trust one another.

Allow silence to happen, even if is uncomfortable.

Encourage quiet people to speak, but allow them to be silent if they wish.

If you're talking too much, remember, you don't have to say everything.
> If someone else is talking too much, help them to remember the same thing.

Exercises in Becoming Present to the Group

Our experience has shown us that it is important for members of a small group to take time at the beginning of their gathering to relax and become centered; it is a time to let go of the distractions of the day. So often as we run out the door to our SCF meeting, we leave a crying child, a list of "to-dos," a disgruntled somebody, a sink full of dishes or a myriad of other distractions. The same is often true for our entire day; we may be thinking of an unpleasant interaction with a fellow employee, a mistake made at work, some information we received during a dentist or doctor visit. These distractions can keep us from being in touch with ourselves or from being fully a part of the group. For that reason, we believe that it is important to set aside a few moments to become present to self and the group. The first part of every meeting helps further this process. In talking about some distraction, something that went wrong, a success or a joyful event, a person is able to leave it behind and focus on the "now." We have also found that during this introductory time, people often talk about more than just the day. If something exciting or difficult has happened since the group last met, people seem to find it helpful to let the group know. As groups continue to meet on an ongoing basis, it is important to let one another know what is going on in their day-to-day life.

We have included four different focusing exercises that can be used or adapted as needed. You will know your group best, and can decide what works best. It seems too, that different times call for different ways of focusing a group. We encourage each facilitator to be creative in how this is done. Many books are available as an aid for this type of centering. Some are listed in the bibliography.

Focus Exercise One

Allow each person in the group to take two to three minutes to become in touch with their own body, its tensions, feelings, joys and distractions. Relaxing the muscles is very important. We all lead busy lives and are often so much on the run. We are not aware of being tied in knots or sometimes of being distracted. The following exercise works very well in getting people ready to speak and to listen to one another. This is to be read *very* slowly, with significant pauses and with enough enunciation to be heard, but not with so much intensity as to be a distraction.

Sit straight in your chair. If your clothing, shoes or glasses are tight, you may want to loosen them. Close your eyes and turn your palms up in your lap. Be aware of your breathing. Savor each breath. Become aware of the muscles of your neck. Let your head tip forward just a bit and let it gently roll from side to side. Tighten your shoulders a bit—hold that for a few seconds, then relax. As you do this feel the tensions leave your body. Let your body take in a deep breath, breathe in peace and tranquillity. As you breathe out, let any distraction of the day become more and more distant. Do this two or three times. Make a fist with your hand, let it tighten. Picture yourself embracing the moment, holding it and being a part of it. As you relax your fist, feel the energy pull you into the presence of everyone gathered here this evening. Allow your heart to soften so as to be entirely present, your ears to become keen to hear what others say, and your eyes to be alert to take in all that is. Take a few more moments to listen to your breathing, to relax, and when you are ready, become present to this group.

Focus Exercise Two

After people have talked about their day, and have done some connection with one another, suggest to them that we are going to do a centering exercise. The following is to be read very slowly, with significant pauses and with enough enunciation to be heard, but not with so much intensity as to be a distraction.

Please become quiet, close your eyes and become aware of your breathing; only your body, and your breathing. Let outside distractions, and noises fade away and allow yourself simply to "be." (Follow this with at least one minute of quiet. Allow the quiet to relax the group.) Make the decision to be involved at your very best level of communication within the group. Come back to the group, and when you are ready open your eyes and become present to this group.

Focus Exercise Three

After people have shared their day, announce that we are going to do a centering exercise. The following is to be read very slowly, with significant pauses and with enough enunciation to be heard, but not with so much intensity as to be a distraction.

Take a moment to connect with that quiet place within yourself. To do that you may want to take a few deep, slow breaths. As you do this let your hands become open in your lap. Lift them just a bit—enough so that they are held out in front of you. Let your eyes focus on your hands. Reflect for a moment on the work these hands have done, just during this day. What act of mercy have they performed, who has been touched by these hands?

Think of other hands that have helped you, perhaps parents, teachers, brothers or sisters, other members of this group tonight. Let a memory come to your mind of just one set of hands. Don't analyze that memory, cherish it, let it become more real, more present now. Now, take that memory and ever so delicately pull it to your heart and feel its warmth. Give thanks for those hands. (Pause) When you are ready come back to the group.

Focus Exercise Four

This exercise will help us focus our thoughts. The relaxation process will help us all listen to the reflection and become present for the rest of the discussion. Read the following slowly.

Get comfortable in your chair.
For good listening, the posture of the body is important.
Sit straight, put your feet on the floor (pause slightly
　　after each line).
Close your eyes.
Rest your hands in your lap, palms up,
　　become aware of your breathing.
As you breathe in, let your breathing relax you.
As you breathe out, let go of the distractions of the day.
As you breathe in, feel your shoulders and neck relax.
As you breathe out, turn loose of any frustrations that
　　are drawing you from this moment.
As you breathe in, let us listen to our reflection.

Gatherings for Contact Persons

The contact persons are not to be seen as "mini-pastors" or as pastoral facilitators of the groups. Rather, they are liaisons among the SCFs and between the SCFs and the parish on an ongoing basis.

Gatherings with the contact persons allow the staff to communicate with the SCFs concerning the dialogue progress of the groups, and the quality of the interaction with other groups and with the parish. They also allow the groups to communicate to the staff any problems they see with the groups or with the parish.

These gatherings should eventually take place 2–3–4 times a year. When you are just getting SCFs going it might be enough to meet 1–2 times a year with the contact persons. Don't try to get everything up and running the first year. Whatever you do some people will enjoy and some people will drop by the wayside. Don't wait to get everything into place. And above all don't expect things to go along without a hitch. What is needed most is patience and persistence. The people who meet in the SCFs should be the major focus. Other connections, events, etc., will come in time.

A Sample Outline for a Gathering of Contact Persons with the Parish Staff

An evening gathering for the contact persons should involve some teaching by the parish staff on the nature of Small Communities of Faith, and how they connect people and connect to the larger church.

7:30   Gathering and Overview of the meeting.
Introductions and Prayer (as part of the prayer we suggest
reading 1 Cor 12:12–20 or some similar passage).

7:45   Pastor, preferably, or another staff person speaks about scripture
and the vision and practice of small communities. Comments on
Paul's image of the mystical body of Christ and our ability to
experience such a real connection with other parishioners and the
whole church.
This is an important place to connect tradition, scripture, and
pastoral wisdom. It sets the direction for the parish and connects
the small groups to the whole.

8:00   Ask the people to talk in twos about what they just heard.

8:10   Ask people to form one large group for a discussion about how
SCFs do or do not help me feel more connected with other
people and with the entire parish.

8:30   Ask people to turn back to the same person they talked with before
and as a pair join another pair to discuss "How can the groups
help us, individually, and as a group be more connected with each
other and with the parish?"

8:40   Ask each group to put its ideas on newsprint. These should be
available beforehand and passed out at this time along with
markers—black, blue and red are always readable.

8:45   Ask each group to hang its newsprint on the
walls around the room, and ask
everyone to walk around and read all the comments from the
different groups.

8:50   The pastor, or staff person for the evening, comments on what the
groups have come up with, and connects all this back to the
beginning prayer and talk. This is a time to articulate again the
vision of what we're about as church. Send the people away
energized.

8:55   Closing prayer on the theme to recommit to our vision and
purpose, ending with a song.

9:00   Refreshments

9:30   Dispersal and cleanup

Networking

The Parish Level

One of the big fears of any pastor or staff of a parish is that small communities of faith will turn inward and lose the idea of the common good for the parish, the church and the world. Often the bonding that happens within a group creates such a wonderful sense of belonging that the group, without noticing it, becomes focused simply on one another. First of all, we suggest that the pastor and every member of the parish staff (insofar as possible) join a different SCF and also that each group have a contact person. We don't envision that this person be the leader or the facilitator of the group, because we encourage the groups to rotate the responsibility of running the evening, hosting and bringing refreshments. Every person of the group develops co-responsibility as a co-leader. However it is important that there be a contact person and that the coordinating person of the communities for the parish can check in to see how the group is doing. This contact person is invaluable in giving feedback about the progress of the group, how the questions and process are going, if there are any problems. They also are important in the coordination of large gatherings of the SCFs in the parish, or region.

Because SCFs can get caught up with themselves and look only inward we recommend that all of the SCFs of the parish gather in a central place (e.g., parish hall) two or three times a year. Since we suggest segments of seven- or eight-week small group gatherings we have found it beneficial to schedule a parish gathering close to the middle of this time. Each SCF would best skip that week's meetings in favor of the larger gathering. Most people, although not everyone, can shift their personal schedule if the notice of the general meeting is scheduled far enough in advance. The energy level at these general meetings can be high, if they are well planned, and the desire to reach out is much easier to focus at this time. Because these larger meetings are important and profitable we find that people don't mind planning an extra evening into their schedules. We have waited until the end of the seven- or eight-week segments to do a gathering, and it seems that some of the momentum is lost; the mindset is for a break, schedules seem to be tighter as more social gatherings are important at certain seasons. Therefore the attendance has been less. It is most beneficial to have a theme for these gatherings; such as Thanksgiving in the fall, Mardi Gras in the winter and Cinco de Mayo in the spring. You may have special themes for your particular parish.

The reason for these gatherings is varied.

1) It will help each small group to focus outward to other groups and the whole parish.

2) It will be a time for staffs to get a sense about how the process has been going.

3) Groups may want to ask questions from their perspective or to share an insight with other groups.

4) This gives every group a chance to talk with others about what they are discovering about themselves through their group.

5) It is also good to have the chance for people to interact with others in the parish who have similar interests. Most likely they will find that even though they are a part of a small group their experience is different because of the uniqueness of each group.

6) Bringing all the groups together helps to connect with the parish and to allow the pastor or a member of the staff to do some teaching about community, faith, social justice, sharing talents and gifts.

7) People who do not belong to a small community can be invited to these sessions as an introduction to the small group process. They experience firsthand what it's like and can express an interest in joining a group. We advise that persons be added only at the beginning of sets of sessions.

We have found that this gathering works best with the components of a meal, prayer, teaching in some manner, sharing with people from other small groups as well as a chance for each small group to briefly gather to touch base. A twilight retreat evening is good for the process.

In the following pages we have included three examples of parish gatherings which we have found useful. You may use these as they are or you may want to modify them for your particular concerns or parish. We also would encourage you to be creative in planning your own, especially around local celebrations or events.

Parish Small Community of Faith Evenings

#1

A Plan for Thanksgiving Large Communal Evening

6:30   Arrival and socializing
6:40   Prayer before meal; have each table read a stanza from the following.

Thanksgiving Prayer

Come, let us welcome the feast of Thanksgiving with joy and with light.
Light is the symbol of the divine.
The Lord is our light and our salvation.
May the light of gratitude burn brightly in our hearts and around this table,
    not only on the feast of Thanksgiving but at all meals.
In the silence of our hearts, let each of us give thanks
    for all the many gifts that are ours.

Let us also be mindful of those today who are without food and a home.
And let us remember those whom we love who are not now
>   present at our table.

Lord of Gifts, from your holy heart has come a flood of gifts to us.
With uplifted hearts, we have gathered around this table to thank you
>   with prayer and with the worship of feasting.

We are grateful not only for the gifts of life itself, but for all the gifts
>   of friendship, love, devotion and forgiveness that we have shared.
On this feast of giving thanks, Lord God, we thank you for showing us
>   how to return thanks by lives of service, by deeds of hospitality,
>   by kindness to a stranger and by concern for each other.

We are most grateful, this feast day, for the way you, our hidden God,
>   have become visible to us in one another,
>   in countless daily gifts and in the marvels of creation.
Come, Lord of Gifts, and bless our table and all the food of this feast.
Let us thank the Lord, today and all days. Amen
>   edited from *Prayers for the Domestic Church* by Edward Hays, p. 116

All Toast: Happy Thanksgiving!

6:45   Dinner
>   Each regular group brings various items for a Thanksgiving dinner, including
>   turkey, dressing, etc. (this is coordinated beforehand).

7:15   Large group gathering
>   Centering…and reading from the *Wizard of Oz* as follows:
>   Use one of the regular focus exercises

The scarecrow and the Tin Woodsman and the Lion now thanked the Good Witch earnestly for her kindness, and Dorothy exclaimed, "You are beautiful! But you have not yet told me how to get back to Kansas."

"Your silver shoes will carry you over the desert," replied Glinda. If you had known their power you could have gone back to your Aunt Em the very first day you came to this country."

"But then I should not have had my wonderful brains!" cried the Scarecrow. "I might have passed my whole life in the farmer's cornfield."

"And I should not have had my lovely heart," said the Tin Woodsman. "I might have stood and rusted in the forest till the end of the world."

"And I should have lived a coward forever," declared the Lion, "and no beast in all the forest would have had a good word to say to me."

"This is all true," said Dorothy, "and I am glad I was of use to these good friends. But now that each of them has had what each desired most, and each is happy in having a kingdom to rule besides, I think I should like to go back to Kansas."

"The silver shoes," said the Good Witch, "have wonderful powers. And one of the most curious things about them is that they can carry you to any place in the world in three steps, and each step will be made in the wink of an eye. All you have to do is to knock the heels together three times and command the shoes to carry you to wherever you wish to go."

"If that is so," said the child joyfully, "I will ask them to carry me back to Kansas at once." She threw her arms around the Lion's neck and kissed him, patting his big head tenderly. Then she kissed the Tin Woodsman, who was weeping in a way most dangerous to his joints. But she hugged the soft stuffed body of the Scarecrow in her arms instead of kissing his painted face, and found she was crying herself at this sorrowful parting from her loving comrades.

Glinda the Good stepped down from her silver throne to give the little girl a good-bye kiss, and Dorothy thanked her for all the kindness she had shown to her friends and herself.

Dorothy now took Toto up solemnly in her arms, and having said one last good-bye she clapped the heels of her shoes together three times, saying. "Take me home to Aunt Em!"

from *The Wonderful Wizard of Oz* by L. Frank Baum

7:30	Small Group process

Hand out prepared questions.

1. Tell a story about something in your life about which you are most thankful.
2. Dorothy probably could have clicked her heels together at any time during her stay in the Land of Oz and gone home. We all have a bit of the cowardly/courageous lion, the heartless/loving Tin Man, the brainless/intelligent Straw Man. Are there things you wished for all your life, yet were afraid to take the risk or the steps necessary to make it happen?
3. If your wish had come true, what would you have missed?

7:55   Large group discussions and further questions

8:15   Wrap-up and summary talk by staff person. (Make sure to summarize the good, comfortable feelings generated, something accomplished and the energy and excitement for the future.)

8:25   Closing prayer.

8:30   Cleanup, socializing and leave taking.

2

A Winter–Mardi Gras Celebration

6:30   People arrive and mingle

6:40   Prayer before meal

Lord our God, on this eve of Ash Wednesday, we ask that You
    bless our celebration on the feast of Mardi Gras.
Bless our table, our food and wine, as well as all of us who sit
    about this feast day table.
Come, Gracious Lord, and join us at this feast as we prepare
    to join Your Son, Jesus, by prayerfully entering into these
    forty days of Lent.
As the food and wine of this feast give nourishment and strength
    to our bodies and spirits, so may we, during this coming
    season of Lent, give strength and support to each other
    and to all who accompany us on this pilgrimage of prayer
    from Ash Wednesday to the Easter Celebrations.
As this Lenten roadway causes us to reflect upon the death of our
    Lord, may we also remember His victory in His
    resurrection from the dead.
May this dinner, on the eve of the day of ashes, be a joyful
    foretaste of the rebirth and new life that is the promise
    of the Feast of the Resurrection.
Together, for the final time before these forty days, let us sing
    the ancient song of joyful victory: Alleluia!
                    from *Prayers for the Domestic Church* by Edward Hays, p. 94

6:45   Dinner
7:15   Transition—clearing of dinner
7:20   Centering followed by reflection
            Use one of the centering exercises, pp. 31–33.

Lenten Psalm of the Royal Road

Lenten road, four-laned royal way, lead me to my Beloved in these
    forty days of prayerful pilgrimage.
Royal and rich is the roadway of earnest prayer and worship, and
    blessed are those who travel it. They will find in the cave of
    their hearts the One whom they seek.
Royal and treasure-filled is the lane of study and reading, hours spent
    in feeding the soul with food of knowledge, insights into the
    divine nature.
Royal and compassionate is the avenue of alms-giving and of working
    for the poor. Twice-blessed are those who give of self and
    treasure as a Lenten work of worship.

Royal and fertile with life is the lane of discipline, fast and abstinence
    which makes all disciples aware of their dependence on the
    truest ground of being, carrying every pilgrim homeward bound.
Spirit of holiness, come to our aid, that we might walk with prayerful
    passion during these forty days on all four lanes of heaven's
    Lenten Royal Road.

                        from *Prayers for a Planetary Pilgrim* by Edward Hays, p. 138

7:25   Break into small groups different from the regular groups.

Hand out and dialogue about the following questions.
1.   Tell of a particularly significant Lenten season in your life.
What was different about it?
2.   As a Lenten pilgrim, what roadway or lane are you considering
as Ash Wednesday nears; i.e., prayer-worship, discipline,
abstinence-fast, study, reading, knowledge, almsgiving, working
for the poor? What do you hope it will do for your spiritual life?

7:40   Regather into large group.
Ask one person to be prepared beforehand to tell a Lenten story.
Then ask, "What stories do you have from the past that you
would like to share?"

7:55   Closing prayer
This can be short, done by the pastor or some parish leader

8:00   Dessert and socializing

#3

A Spring–Cinco de Mayo Celebration

6:30   Gathering and socializing
6:40   Opening Prayer
Song: *Be Not Afraid*, Bob Dufford, S.J., NALR
Short reading of the story of Cinco de Mayo

Following a brief civil war over the Constitution of 1857, the defeated conservative faction of Mexico turned to Europe for support. With hopes of creating a Latin League between Mexico, Spain, France and other European nations, the conservatives and Europeans looked for an excuse for intervention in Mexico. This chance came when the liberal Mexican government suspended payments on loans made by France and England. At the beginning of 1862 the French army began their march toward Mexico City.

On May 5, the French army of about 6000 men advanced on the city of Puebla where the Mexican army of equal number waited at Fort Guadeloupe. Following an artillery bombardment in which only a few shells landed in the fort the French infantry moved in. Their advance was met with heavy Mexican musket fire and artillery. By late afternoon a heavy downpour of rain had begun. Faced with heavy casualties the French army was forced to retreat. The Mexican army spent their night celebrating their victory by cheering and singing Mexican songs, for they had just defeated in battle an army which had the international reputation of being the best army in the world.

edited from *Maximilian and Juarez* by Jasper Ridley,
Ticknor and Fields, 1992, pp. 96–102

Prayer:

Lord and Divine Protector,
We are gathered this evening to celebrate
    independence, and victory over difficult odds.
This is an evening to reflect about the time in history when
    the Mexican people defeated the French;
        but it is also an evening to think of our own
        victories—both large and small.
At time in our lives we feel helpless and small
    before powers that sometimes
    seem beyond our control and abilities.
At time, everything seems dark and dangerous,
    yet we place our trust in You, our Lord and God.
Sheltered here within our parish community
    we are aware that we are shielded by Your love
    against all that might harm us.
Tonight we lift up our hearts
    in gratitude and praise to you
You are a God who brings forth good things
    from the dark times of life.
Bless are you, Lord our God,
    who saves those who trust in you. Amen
            adapted from *Prayers for the Domestic Church* by Edward Hays, p. 39

6:45   Dinner

7:20   Large circle or concentric circles around a center
        Reflection: (1 Samuel 17:41–50)

        With his shield bearer marching before him, the Philistine also advanced closer and
        closer to David. When he had sized David up, and seen that he was youthful, and
        ruddy, and handsome in appearance, he held him in contempt. The Philistine said to

David, "Am I a dog that you come against me with a staff?" Then the Philistine cursed David by his gods and said to him, "Come here to me, and I will leave your flesh for the birds of the air and the beasts of the field." David answered him: "You come against me with sword and spear and scimitar, but I come against you in the name of the LORD of hosts, the God of the armies of Israel that you have insulted. Today the LORD shall deliver you into my hand; I will strike you down and cut off your head. This very day I will leave your corpse and the corpses of the Philistine army for the birds of the air and the beasts of the field; thus the whole land shall learn that Israel has a God. All this multitude, too shall learn that it is not by sword or spear that the LORD saves. For the battle is the LORD'S, and he shall deliver you into our hands."

The Philistine then moved to meet David at close quarters, while David ran quickly toward the battle line in the direction of the Philistine. David put his hand into the bag and took out a stone, hurled it with the sling, and struck the Philistine on the forehead. The stone embedded itself in his brow, and he fell prostrate on the ground. [Thus David overcame the Philistine with sling and stone; he struck the Philistine mortally, and did it without a sword.]

7:25   Gather into small groups (not a person's regular group) and dialogue concerning the following questions. (You may prepare and hand out.)
1.   David and Goliath is a story from Jewish history, Cinco de Mayo is a story from Mexican history. Tell a story from your family history about victory over difficult times, oppression, etc.
2.   Tell of a time when you were faced with a situation that seemed insurmountable yet you were able to get through it, overcome it, or feel victorious.
3.   How has God and our faith community been a part of getting you through difficult times?

7:45   Regather into a large group and dialogue about the following questions.
1.   In the small group we talked about how God or our small communities got us through difficult times. Have there been other groups, or the parish, that have helped you get through difficult times. Tell a story about it.
2.   We are almost through this year. Some of you have been in small groups for varying times. What impact has the small group had on your life, your faith, your spiritual journey?

8:00   Closing Song: *The Spirit is a Movin'*, Carey Landry, NALR

8:05   Dessert

8:15   Cleanup and leave taking

Regional Gatherings

We have also found that by simply staying within our parish boundaries, we can also become inward and complacent. As the years pass and SCFs continue to grow, the parish is transformed, and it is important to share that with others in our immediate area: those in our parish cluster, deanery or region. The benefit of going beyond our parish boundaries is manifold. It gives us a chance to meet new people, to possibly change our perspective, and experience new ways of "being" for and with one another. It is a wonderful way to share resources, and to make connections with a local dean or bishop of the area. It also seems that these gatherings are a great time to seize the teachable moment for many who are hungering for church teachings in many areas (prayer, social teachings, etc.). To have a theme for a teaching that allows people to focus on questions that will help them internalize the concepts can be very powerful both personally and for a regional gathering.

We have found that late spring or early summer is a good time to have a gathering for a large region. Most regions or dioceses have people who are interested in helping with planning, resources or providing a place to gather.

We have included in this chapter an outline of a recent retreat day that was presented in our region.

Regional Gathering—an Example

This can happen among a cluster of parishes; a deanery, region of the diocese, or the whole diocese.

From Ordinary Time to Extraordinary Presence

(What happens when ordinary people come together.)

12:30–1:05	Registration
1:05–1:10	Greeting
	MCs for the day are responsible for timing/facilitating and leading all sessions
	Gathering information and preview of day
1:10–1:20	Prayer, scripture, song
1:20–1:30	First talk. (The foundations, basic description of what SCFs are, why they are important in our lives and in the church. Set the theme for the day.)
1:30–1:50	Break into two groups
	A) New people (first timers) form one group and meet in a second room. A male/female team should talk 12 minutes about SCFs making connections, RCIA, Renew, etc., 5–7 minute discussion.
	B) Current SCF members meet in interparish small groups, discussion based on first talk, centering on foundations, summarize on newsprint.
1:50–2:00	Everyone return to one large group in the original room
	Hang newsprint…everyone read summaries (newcomers included)

2:00–2:15	Large group discussion…questions
2:15–2:45	Second talk. (Small group process, sacredness of person…group…community as connection to larger church, parish, diocese.)
2:45–3:00	Break…time to continue to read newsprint and talk
3:00–3:10	MCs regather for large group discussion and reaction to talk.
3:10–3:30	Third talk…(mystery of God…time out of time…how do we deal with these…mystery/sacredness of what happens in community…how did Jesus teach us to deal with the mystery of life.)
3:30–3:45	Personal reflection…quiet journaling. How does God reveal to me, to us, through the events and experiences of our lives and community? The ordinary does reveal the extraordinary mystery and sacredness of life.
3:45-4:10	Gather back to original small group to discuss personal reactions… questions…comments Newcomers…back to the other room. All talk in threes about talks and reflections (6 min.) Share together with the male/female leaders
4:10–4:15	Regroup to one large group
4:15–4:35	Large group reflections…discussions…comments
4:35–4:50	Speakers (M/F) do a wrap-up…summary…5 min. each One person from newcomers and one person from current SCF give a two-minute witness talk.
4:50–5:00	Break
5:00–6:00	Mass…liturgy of Ordinary People
6:20–7:00	Dinner
6:30	Evaluations (spoken and written) during the last part of dinner

National Level

The resources at these gatherings are almost limitless: people come to these convocations with a variety of experiences of small groups; the liturgies are inspiring and renewing; the resources for materials are many. There are probably many such groups formed around the country, but three are organized nationally: Buena Vista, which designs their activities for the typical SCF member; the National Alliance of Parishes Restructuring into Communities, which works with the pastor and parish staff; and The North American Forum for Small Christian Communities, which is mainly for diocesan staff persons. The addresses of offices are included in the bibliography.

How to Plan Your Own Sessions

In years 2 and 3 there is one "do-it-yourself" session in each set of sessions. We give a theme, some definitions, and a process for developing questions within the session, including the discussion questions. By the time you reach year 4 you will know how to write questions that draw out the life experiences of the members and do not become too ethereal or theoretical. You will also have learned that any material will be suitable for a starting point, and that all things will be connected with tradition and with scripture. Scripture and Catholic tradition will have become alive in the present by this process.

A good way to begin is to look at the values in the back of this book. Select three that seem to be important but not receiving sufficient attention in your group (choose one each from Basic, Growth, and Motivational). Look at the readings from the tradition (also in the appendix) and select one that seems to fit each value. Look also at the scriptures for something that fits the theme. Something from scripture and tradition are not always necessary. Divide up into committees and plan one session per committee. In an evening you ought to be able to plan 3 or 4 sessions. That way there will be no homework.

In the third session of the winter year 4 set you will be able to plan the remaining open sessions for the year. Decide how you want to plan, and break up into the appropriate committees.

By the time you reach year 5 you will be ready to take an overall view toward planning sessions for your group, keeping in mind the cycles of liturgical and secular life, and the normal dynamics inherent in our society. You can use this book, other books, almost anything as resources for the elements of value, process, questions, extra readings, evaluation and prayer. Remember that you are planning now for the rest of your lives—year 5 and beyond!

This process of dialogue in small groups will have prepared members to realize "We Are the Church." We are always in union with other parish small groups, contributing to the larger deanery, region and diocese. We also will be working in our part of the world so that all people may see how they love and support one another and that the work of the Lord continues. The poor, the homeless, the abandoned, the rejected, the suffering are all receiving compassion and care. May we continue to dream, to dialogue and Be Church for the world.

Small Community of Faith Evaluation

This is the end of our seven-week experience of small groups. Would you like to be a part of small groups for the next set of sessions? If yes, please provide the information below after discussing it with your group. (We do encourage groups to stay together, if possible, so discussion can be more effective as the group grows together.)

Name:
Phone:
best day to meet:
    2nd choice
best time of day
    2nd choice

Think back over the past few weeks. Do you have any closing thoughts or comments on your experience?

Do you have any suggestions for improvement?

Did some sessions work better than others for you? Why?

Do you know anyone who might be interested in small communities of faith? Please invite them to sign up for the next set of sessions or provide their name and we will contact them. Thank you.

CHAPTER 4

In this chapter there are three sets of seven sessions for a first year. We recommend the groups meet in these three different times for seven consecutive weeks. Most people's busy lives can adjust to that. Each of the sessions is clearly marked and ready to use.

YEAR 1 - F - 1

Theme: Welcoming

Facilitator: Hospitality is an important part of all sessions, particularly this initial session. Be a welcoming person! Try to always address each person by name. You may want to allow more or less time for some parts of the session, depending on the response of the group. However, be aware that it is always better to finish a section before everyone has said everything they want to say. It is important that each person say something. If you lengthen one part then another needs to be shortened. People need to feel cared for by getting started on time and ending on time. That's what they were expecting and will appreciate. Always keep in mind the overall time line, so that everyone will be more than willing to return knowing that their time commitment will be respected.

Gathering Time—Welcoming and Sharing (12–15 Minutes)

Facilitator: Make sure that the people are greeted. Get everyone seated as soon as it is comfortable. Start off by announcing the theme for this session. Then take the first few minutes to ask each person to introduce themselves and talk just a minute about themselves. There can then be comments about any important events of their day to this point. This is a time for everyone to come to feel at ease with the group, and begin to get acquainted.

Facilitator: At this point read the Guidelines for Sharing, pp. 30–31, and at the end let anyone ask any question they might have about what it said. Later on there will be plenty of time to figure out much more about what it means point by point. Don't spend much time other than reading it. Explain the outline for the session: We begin with a reading for reflection, followed by a discussion or dialogue with questions for guidance. We will wrap up by saying how we think things went and end with refreshments. The reflection at the beginning is not for discussion; rather it serves as a focal point for us to become present to this place and time. Ask someone to read the reflection, with a few moments pause at the end.

A Reading from *The New Yorker* by Leopold Tyrmand cited in *Let's Pray* by Br. Charles Reutemann, F.S.C.

The reception was chic, and people communicated with no hesitation. For a few minutes I faced a tall, well-dressed man with a superb mustache; he was related to me only through the metaphysics of the cocktail party. He looked quite Waspish, and was endowed with the special dash of boredom and cheerfulness that characterizes some members of the American upper class. He mumbled a small something. I had difficulty catching what he said. "Where are you from?" he asked, almost indifferently. I told him where I was from.

"What are you doing in this country?" he asked. I told him what I was doing here. "When are you going back?" he pursued, apparently without any deeper interest than to keep up the conversation. "It's hard to say," I answered. "Perhaps in twenty or thirty years. I've applied for permanent residence here." "Well," he said, "welcome aboard." This open acceptance was unexpected, and I must have looked startled, because he added, "You know, after all, all of us came to this country sometime. Three generations earlier or later—what does it matter? Let's drift along together."

(Pause for a few moments)

Small Group Discussion (20–25 Minutes)

Facilitator: Ask people to take a few moments and reflect on the questions in silence. Then ask persons to break up into groups of three with persons they do not know—at least very well. If the whole group is uneven, form groups of three and two. Advise them of the time for the talking and that you will give them a two-minute warning before the final finishing

time. Remind them that the point is not to answer the question but to use it as a point of reference in telling something about themselves. Each person needs to have time to talk, yet should not be "put on the spot" by pointed questions from someone else. Use the following questions for reflection and dialogue.

1. Reflect on and talk about an event you attended where you did *not* feel welcome. Tell what the event was, the people involved (don't use names) and how they interacted with you, and how you responded.

2. Talk about a time you did feel welcomed. Why and what made the difference? How did you respond? Because of the interaction, did you feel better about yourself? How would you describe that feeling?

3. What happens in a relationship as people get to know one another better? Is there a difference in the trust level? What happens?

Merge Groups (25–30 Minutes)

Facilitator: Ask two groups to merge for further discussion. Depending on the number there may be unequally sized groups. Ask them to talk about the same question again.

Large Group Discussion (15 Minutes)

Facilitator: After having given them a two-minute warning to finish their discussions, ask the groups to come together into one large group again. Facilitate a discussion of the following questions.

1. What story from your group did you identify with? What did you learn from it?
2. What did you learn or recognize from your experience, or from listening to others?

Wrap-up and Evaluation (5–7 Minutes)

Facilitator: Encourage people to talk about how they think the session went, e.g., what do you think about it? How did you feel about it? Was everyone involved, did we encourage each other? Be sure to allow time to close with any final questions people may have or any comments you want to make. Announce the theme, "Listening," for the next gathering. Confirm the date, time and place for the next meeting. If necessary make sure directions are clear. Ask who will host, at their home, apartment or dorm room. We recommend rotating meeting places and all the functions. Who will facilitate, if you have not agreed to do it for the first 3–4 weeks to get people used to it? Who will bring refreshments? Remember they are to be simple and easily handled.

Refreshments (1/2 hour)

Facilitator: Make sure that these are available immediately (maybe even set out in advance, or have someone assigned to take care of it). It is important that these be simple and that everyone can eat, socialize and leave within the time framework.

YEAR 1 - F - 2

Theme: Listening

Facilitator: The theme on listening is to help each person in the group (1) to be at ease in telling his/her own story because others are listening, (2) learn to listen well to others as he/she in turn tells his/her story, (3) begin to internalize what the other person is saying.

Gathering Time—Welcoming and Sharing (5–10 Minutes)

Facilitator: Welcoming and hospitality are always very important, most especially at the beginning of a group's gathering. Make sure that you and the host carry this out with class and grace. Have people talk about their day, how they are doing, what's on their mind for the moment. This time is simply to help each one feel at ease with the group and to begin to "refocus" from the busy day. Announce the theme of the session. Briefly review the Guidelines for Sharing, pp. 30–31, by reading all or parts of it. Remind people that there will be a short reading for reflection, again to help focus on being present, not for discussion. Ask someone to do the reading.

A Reading from *The Life of Dialogue* by Martin Buber cited in *Let's Pray* by Br. Charles Reutemann, F.S.C.

Genuine conversation is most often found in the dialogue between two persons, but it also occurs occasionally in a dialogue of several voices. Not everyone present has to speak this dialogue to be genuine, but no one can be there as a mere observer. Each must be ready to share with the others, and no one who really takes part can know in advance that he/she will not have something to say. Genuine dialogue can thus be spoken or silent. Its essence lies in the fact that "each participant really has in mind the other or others in their present and particular being and turns to them with the intention of establishing a living mutual relation between him-self and them." The essential element of gen-uine dialogue, therefore, is "seeing the other" or "experiencing the other side."

"Experiencing the other side" means to feel an event from the side of the person one meets as well as from one's own side. It is an inclusiveness which realizes the other person in the actuality of his being....[The elements of this inclusiveness] are, first, a relation, of no matter what kind between two persons; second, an event experienced by them in common, in which at least one of them actively participates; and, third, the fact that this one person, without forfeiting anything of the felt reality of his activity, at the same time lives through the common event from the standpoint of the other.

(Pause for a few moments of reflection.)

Small Group Discussion (5–7 Minutes)

Facilitator: Ask people to read over the question, think about it for a minute and then begin a dialogue with one other per-son. Let the group know that after each question, it will then turn back to the large group for further discussion. Ask people to turn to another person, preferably someone they do not know, at least not well, and talk about the following question.

1. Relate a story from last summer of something good, exciting, that hap-pened to you. (2–3 minutes each)

Large Group Discussion (15–18 Minutes)

Facilitator: Ask the people to gather into a large group and ask each person to intro-duce the person they just spoke with by telling their partner's story to the large group.

Small Group Discussion (5–8 Minutes)

Facilitator: Ask the people to form different (new) groups of two and talk about the following question.

2. Tell about a difficult time you experi-enced this summer, such as a disap-pointment, a hurt, something that didn't go as planned.

Large Group Discussion (15–18 Minutes)

Facilitator: Ask the people to regather into one large group. Ask each person to relate his/her partner's story to the group, try-ing to tell not only the details but other things observed or heard, e.g., body lan-guage, emotions that seemed to be beneath the words, eye expression, etc.

Small Group Discussion (5–8 Minutes)

Facilitator: Ask people to now go back to the last partner they had and talk about the following point.

3. Talk about how you thought each of you did in telling your story. More impor-tantly, tell the other person what you experienced as you listened to them tell their story. (We often are not aware of the impact we have on another person by relating a story from our own life.)

Large Group Discussion (5–10 Minutes)

Facilitator: Ask the people to gather again into one large group and dialogue about the following questions.

1. What things have you learned about listening?

2. What are some listening skills that you became more aware of during the session?

Wrap-up and Evaluation (3–5 Minutes)

Facilitator: Get everyone talking about how things went, comments they would like to make or any suggestions. Announce the theme for next week, "Feeling Safe and Accepted." Confirm the place and date of the next session, any directions necessary. Who will host, facilitate and bring refreshments? Remind people that everyone in the group is co-responsible for the group and should eventually plan on rotating to all the differing service positions. You can offer to aid or coach someone through the first time.

Refreshments (1/2 hour)

Facilitator: Make sure that these are served quickly and that people are able to socialize but able to leave within the agreed upon time. Enjoy!

YEAR 1 - F - 3

Theme: Feeling Safe and Accepted

Gathering Time—Welcoming and Sharing (5–10 Minutes)

Facilitator: Make sure that good welcoming and hospitality happens at the beginning of the session. You might arrive slightly early to help get ready. Ask how they are and what's been happening to them. This is the beginning of letting go of cares and focusing on this time and our conversations.

To further aid this you might ask if people would mind beginning with a focusing exercise. You can read and comment on part of the Guidelines for Sharing, pp. 30–31, that might be good to stress. Remind people of the theme for the session and that after the focusing exercise

there will again be a short reading for reflection, not discussion. Ask someone to do that reading at the end of the focus exercise.

Focus Exercise (2–3 Minutes)

Facilitator: Choose one from pp. 31–33.

A Reading from the Inscription on the Statue of Liberty

Give me your tired, your poor, your huddled masses yearning to be free, the wretched refuse of your teeming shore. Send these, the homeless, tempest tossed to me. I lift my lamp beside the golden door.
(Pause for a few moments of silence and reflection)

A Reading from Mother Teresa, *Something Beautiful for God*

Be kind and merciful. Let no one ever come to you without coming away better and happier. Be the living expression of God's kindness; kindness in your face, kindness in your eyes, kindness in your smile, kindness in your warm greeting. In the slums we are the light of God's kindness to the poor. To the children, to the poor, to all who suffer and are lonely, give always a happy smile—give them not only your care, but also your heart.
(Pause for a moment)

Small Group Discussion (30 Minutes)

Facilitator: Ask people to form into groups of three, preferably with people they don't know well, and talk about the following questions.

1. Have you ever been without a job or without an income? What did this do to your sense of security (paying bills, putting food on the table)? Have you ever taken on a big debt? Car? House? How did you feel? What were the excitements? What were the fears?

2. In work, school, home, community, what kinds of stress do you experience to be successful, "number one"? Is there a pressure to perform by your manager, professor or your peers? Do you feel a pressure in yourself to be at the top or to compete?

3. What is a symbol of security to you (house, car, money, etc.)? Do you worry about losing any of these?

4. Do you ever feel the need to be alone? What do you do?

5. Was there a time when your residence was threatened (by a disaster—fire, flood, etc.)? If that were happening right now, what three items would you grab, assuming your family/room-mates were safe?

Large Group Discussion (35 Minutes)

Facilitator: Ask the people to come together in one large group and dialogue about the following questions.

1. What were some of the significant symbols of security that you heard expressed in your group?

2. In terms of security, what do you think is important? Did you learn something about yourself that you weren't aware of?

3. What were some of the stresses that people experienced to be successful or to perform?

4. What were some of the things that people talked about when they wanted to be alone?

5. What were some of the things that people would rescue in case of a disaster?

6. Do we treat all with the same outlook?

Remember Mother Teresa's quote (reread if necessary). In meeting with those less fortunate, do we try to have them leave us better and happier from the encounter?

Wrap-up and Evaluation (7–10 Minutes)

Facilitator: Facilitate a discussion of how the session went. Is there something a person would like to say, any question, comment. Announce the theme for next session, "Being Liked by Others." Confirm all the details: time, place, directions, who facilitates, hosts and who will bring refreshments.

Refreshments (1/2 hour)

Facilitator: Help see that refreshments are served quickly and that people socialize but are able to leave on time.

YEAR 1 - F - 4

Theme: Being Liked by Others

Gathering Time—Welcoming and Sharing (5–10 Minutes)

Facilitator: Make sure good welcoming and hospitality are done. This involves getting people talking about how their day has gone, anything they want to say about what they're doing. Announce the theme for the session. You may also want to review some part of the Guidelines for Sharing, pp. 30–31, with any comment or question. Remind people that the reading is to help focus on the theme, but without discussion. Ask some to do the reading at the end of the focus exercise.

Focus Exercise (2–3 Minutes)

Facilitator: Pre-choose one from pp. 31–33.

A Reading from *The Potter's Touch* by William Reiser, S.J.

What, then, is the first grace? The first grace is what becomes fundamental to everything else in human life. It is being loved and accepted by someone before we have come to realize and to appreciate the importance of that gift. For most people, this gift will provide the primary example of a purely free and gracious action on our behalf. In the context of Christian faith, it is to know with the apostle John that God loved us first (1 Jn 4:10). In the context of human relationships, it means being grateful to parents and friends for their love. In the context of our own solitude, first grace means being struck by the utter gratuity of our existence; it stirs us to gladness and gratitude for the sheer fact of being alive. (Pause for a few moments)

Small Group Discussion (30–35 Minutes)

Facilitator: Tell people that there are two sets of questions. After we talk briefly about the first set you'll give them some signal to wind up and begin discussing the second set. That discussion will be the longer part. Remind them of the approximate times and the total time. Ask them to turn to one other person to talk. When they shift at the signal choose a different person to talk with about the last set of questions. As they begin each set take a moment to reflect on the questions before relating experiences.

1. Do you notice people saying "thank you" to you (in the family, at work, among friends, at church activities)? How do you respond?

2. How do you react when others compliment you and how do you feel?

3. Do you tell other people what you like/appreciate about them?

4. Is your first reaction when you see someone to criticize or to praise? Give an example...to think "their clothes don't match, their appearance is different," or to say something positive?

Facilitator: At this point ask the people to change partners.

5. Who have been the most significant people in your life? Tell a story about one of them.

6. Do you tell the significant people in your life that they are important to you? Tell of a time when you did or did not.

7. When a significant person in your life has said something to criticize you, how did you respond? How did they say it—blaming, positive? How did you feel? Because of your reaction, did they change their statement later?

8. What do you expect or want from the significant people in your life right now?

9. What's one thing you would redo in the last week if you had a chance? or in the past?

Large Group Discussion (25 Minutes)

Facilitator: Ask the people to gather into one group and discuss questions 7 and 8 again here.

Wrap-up and Evaluation (5–10 Minutes)

Facilitator: Ask how did it go? Is there anything someone would like to say that he/she didn't have a chance to say yet. Announce the theme for the next session, "Family of Origin and Family of Choice."

Confirm all the details for the next meeting. Who facilitates, hosts, and who brings refreshments?

Refreshments (1/2 hour)

YEAR 1 - F - 5

Theme: Family of Origin and Family of Choice

Gathering Time—Welcoming and Sharing (15 Minutes)

Facilitator: By now the welcoming and hospitality should be going well, since everyone has responsibility for it, but you are the one who checks for any problems. Make sure everyone is feeling comfortable and catching up about the day or week. This brings everyone to the present here and slows them down for a richer time together. Select something from the Guidelines for Sharing, pp. 30–31, that would be good to read and remind people about. Announce the theme for the session and ask for a reader for the reflection reading after the focus exercise.

Focus Exercise (2–3 Minutes)

Facilitator: There are selections pp. 31–33.

A Reading from *The Theology of Presence* by Dick Westley

> Consider the situation of young adults within the family group. Typically, by the time they reach 25–30 years of age, their parents have come to the mid-life passage. Everything in the family is very volatile. The young person is seeking her/his independence, and the parents are having trouble coping with their struggles to find their own identity in a relationship of many years.

> When parents and young adults are simultaneously going through a time of real crisis in their lives, it is very difficult for them to nurture and effectively tend to their intergenerational relationships. Yet, that is the way family life is: people clustered on a journey which takes them in divergent directions, but which keeps them bonded to one another in the most intimate and precarious of relationships. And each family member is asked to discern in his or her own life just how much independence and how much gift of self to the family group is possible. Yes, we tend to romanticize families because of the good things that come from them, but we also know first hand that being a family member remains the most challenging of our roles, both as parent and as offspring.
> (Pause for few moments of reflection)

Small Group Discussion (40 minutes)

Facilitator: Ask the people to form groups of three, two if necessary, and talk about the following questions. As they begin, a little silent reflection on the questions would aid in the personal talking.

1. Who is family for you? Why? Describe.
2. Have your primary relationships changed? When and how were you aware of this?
3. What has been the effect of the relationship change on you? Were others also affected by this?
4. What were your emotions, feelings, thoughts when you moved from your family of origin to other relationships (if this has occurred)?
5. Are home visits different now? Describe. For those with no family to go home to, if you are a parent, consider the relationship with your children when they come home.

6. Who are you closest to in your family? Why?

7. Reflect back on your parents. What changes did you experience over the years as your relationship changed?

Large Group Discussion (20 Minutes)

Facilitator: Ask the people to gather again into one large group. Facilitate a dialogue on the following questions.

1. What were some of the things that struck you as you listened to others tell their stories?

2. Did you gain any insights into your own life, or relationships, as you shared with others?

Wrap-up and Evaluation (5–10 Minutes)

Facilitator: Ask how did we do? Are there any final comments or thoughts? Announce the theme for next week, "Being Supported and Supportive." Confirm all the details about the next session. Who will facilitate, host, and bring refreshments?

Refreshments (1/2 hour)

Facilitator: Make sure that these stay simple and are easily handled so that people can eat, chat and mingle. It is important that the final time frame be observed.

YEAR 1 - F - 6

Theme: Being Supported and Supportive

Gathering Time—Welcoming and Sharing (15 Minutes)

Facilitator: Hospitality should be good by now as everyone is getting used to co-

responsibility for it, but you look for any problems. Make sure people are sharing about their day, week, etc., so that they can set these aside. Announce the theme of the session. Read and comment on some section of the Guidelines for Sharing, pp. 30–31. Ask who will read the reflection after the focus exercise.

Focus Exercise (2–3 Minutes)

Facilitator: There are selections pp. 31–33.

A Reading from *The Velveteen Rabbit* by Margery Williams

"What is REAL?" asked the Rabbit one day, when they were lying side by side near the nursery fender…"Real isn't how you are made," said the Skin Horse, "It's a thing that happens to you.…" "Does it hurt?" asked the Rabbit. "Sometimes," said the Skin Horse, for he was always truthful. "When you are Real you don't mind being hurt." "Does it happen all at once, like being wound up?" he asked, "or bit by bit?" "It doesn't happen all at once," said the Skin Horse. "You become. It takes a long time. That's why it doesn't often happen to people who break easily, or have sharp edges, or who have to be carefully kept. Generally, by the time you are Real, most of your hair has been loved off, and your eyes drop out, and you get loose in the joints and very shabby. But these things don't matter at all, because once you are Real you can't be ugly, except to people who don't understand."

(Pause for a few moments of reflection)

Small Group Discussion (30 Minutes)

Facilitator: Ask the people to form groups of three or two if needed and take a few moments to reflect on the following questions before starting to talk.

1. Who gives you the most physical and emotional support? Tell something about that person.
2. Who gives you the most pain? What do you do to cope with this? Have you ever tried to find other solutions?
3. How do you interact with/trust guests/strangers? Do you often smile, laugh? Have other people ever commented on your interactions with others, either affirming or criticizing?
4. Tell a story of a painful or difficult time. How did you handle it? What did you learn about patience and perseverance? What would you have done differently?

Large Group Discussion (30 Minutes)

Facilitator: Ask the people to form a large group again and dialogue about the following questions. If there is time you might reread some of the small group questions that did not get talked about much.

1. Tell of a time when you felt supported. What was key, and how did you feel?
2. Tell of a time when you were supportive. How did you feel?

Wrap-up and Evaluation (5–6 Minutes)

Facilitator: Ask if there are any last comments or questions. Encourage people to talk about how the session went for them. Announce the theme for next week, "Community Support—Bringing Out the Best in Us." Since the next session will be the last for this set is there anything we want to do especially? This is still early so it probably should be simple, maybe just another 1/2 hour and some more refresh-

ments. As time goes on the group might want to have a final meal as a celebration, or some other social event. This might take a separate meeting.

But for next session confirm all the details. Who facilitates, hosts and brings refreshments?

Refreshments (1/2 hour)

YEAR 1 - F - 7

Theme: Community Support—Bringing Out the Best in Us

Gathering Time—Welcoming and Sharing (5–10 Minutes)

Facilitator: Make the welcoming and hospitality go well. After people have had a chance to talk briefly about their day announce the theme for the session. Ask for someone to read the reflection after the focus exercise.

Focus Exercise (2–3 Minutes)

Facilitator: See selections pp. 31–33.

A Reading from *Redemptive Intimacy* by Dick Westley

We always experience joy when we possess something truly good for us, or which we take to be good for us. Not all our joys are physical, however. There is an exultation, a gladdening in excess of anything physical, which gives us access to a non-physical world of sunniness without sunlight, of sweet things that have no taste, a world of quiet without inertia, of sound without words or music. It is a mysterious kind of joy with no face or figure, no shape or weight, with nothing physical about it other than the fact that it is experienced by someone who is herself physical.

An analysis of such moments invariably reveals that they are the moments of "encounter," in which I really cared for someone else, or they really cared for me. To be sure, we truly rejoice in possessing all manner of things that we need for our physical well-being and comfort or want as signs of our worth, but we love those things the way a dog loves its dinner. Such joys arise from "possessing" particular good things.

(Pause for a few moments)

Small Group Discussion (30 Minutes)

Facilitator: Ask the people to break up into groups of three, or two if necessary, and talk about the following questions.

1. Who are your peers—at work, school, community?

2. Who are your life companions? In what ways do they know you and support you?

3. Are you cooperative—supportive for mutual projects with others? How negative are you? Give an example.

4. In your practice of faith, church, looking for happiness, a more supported/enhanced life, what skills do you need to learn?

Large Group Discussion (20 Minutes)

Facilitator: Ask people to gather in one large group again and lead a dialogue about the final question.

1. What personal strengths have you become aware of by being part of this group?

2. Is there some area of your life in which you need special support? In what way can this group help?

3. What is your favorite memory of being supported/giving support?

Wrap-up and Evaluation (5 Minutes)

Facilitator: Since this is the last session of this set, the parish may want a report from the group. It would be good to take notes at any rate. Ask the people to think back over the last seven sessions and comment on their experience. How has it been? Any suggestions for improvement? Any special comments? If possible give the time, place and date for reconvening for the next set. Or get everyone's name, address and phone number so that contact can be made in plenty of time for beginning again. Make sure that the agreed upon celebration takes place, now or later. You might want to do some special simple prayer to end. We suggest the following.

Pray together:

> Christ in the heart of everyone who
>   thinks of me.
>   Christ in the mouth of everyone who
>   speaks of me,
> Christ in every eye that sees me,
>   Christ in every ear that hears me.
>   Excerpt from *The Breastplate of*
>   *St. Patrick*

Refreshments (1/2 hour)

Or special celebration and final leave taking.

YEAR 1 - W - 1

Theme: Taking Care of Me

Facilitator: Remember that welcoming and hospitality are most important. Throughout the process don't be afraid to allow more or less time for some parts of the process. However, learn to watch for the signals when things are beginning to wane, and move on before people begin to get off the topic, or become restless. The overall time frame is important to keep.

Gathering Time—Welcoming and Sharing (20 Minutes)

Facilitator: Make sure that hospitality and welcoming go well, especially for any new members who may be there. Let people talk about their day, what is happening to them briefly. This is the time to get reacquainted. Announce the theme for the session. A brief introduction time with people just saying their name and one thing about themselves may be important, especially if new people are present. Read the Guidelines for Sharing, pp. 30–31, and ask for questions or comments. Remind people that the reflective reading is to help us focus our thoughts here, and not for discussion. Ask someone to do the reading after the focus exercise.

Focus Exercise (2–3 Minutes)

Facilitator: You should select one from pp. 31–33.

A Reading from "Drowsy in America," *Time* by Anastasia Toufekis, Dec. 17, 1990

At 7 am, or 6 or maybe even 5, the blare of the alarm breaks the night, as another workday dawns. As an arm gropes to stop the noise and the whole body rebels against the harsh call of morning, the thought is almost always the same: I have to get more sleep. That night, after 17 or 18 hours of fighting traffic, facing deadlines and racing the clock, the weary soul collapses into bed once again for an all-too-brief respite. And just before the slide

into slumber, the nagging thought returns: I have to get more sleep.

Millions of Americans make this complaint, but how many do anything about it? Sleep is a biological imperative, but do people consider it as vital as food or drink? Not in today's rock-around-the-clock world. Not in a society in which mothers work, stores don't close, assembly lines never stop, TV beckons all the time, and stock traders have to keep up with the action in Tokyo. For too many Americans, sleep has become a luxury that can be sacrificed or a nuisance that must be endured.

Those who run themselves ragged are often hailed as ambitious comers, while those who insist on getting their rest are dismissed as lazy plodders.

As long as that attitude persists, the national sleep deficit will not be easy to close. What is needed most of all, though, is a fundamental change in Americans' thinking about the necessity of sleep.

Americans have stubbed out cigarettes, laced up exercise shoes and pushed away plates laden with high-cholesterol, high-fat foods. By comparison, choosing to spend some more time abed in blissful oblivion should be attractive. It is a message that is unmistakable: Wake up, America— by getting more sleep.
(Pause for a few moments of reflection)

Small Group Discussion (30 Minutes)

Facilitator: If the group is 10 or less ask people to form groups of two, or three if the group is larger. Make sure newcomers feel welcome as part of this process. Remind people that it isn't necessary to get to all the questions in the session. The purpose is not to answer every question, but to allow sufficient time for each person to tell his/her part of the story without putting anyone on the spot. Let people know that you will give a couple of minutes warning so they can finish their conversation about the following questions. It is good to take a minute and reflect on the questions before beginning to talk.

1. What are your health needs? How have they changed during your life, physically, emotionally, spiritually?

2. Are regular health check-ups important to you? Do you see this as something important to your well-being?

3. When you are not feeling well or under stress, do you recognize where it hurts—physically, emotionally, spiritually? Is there something you can share about this?

4. We all, at times, choose behaviors in life that are not healthy for us. Is there something in your life that you recognize you'd like to work on to bring yourself to fuller health? (This isn't calling for deep disclosure.)

5. How do you respond to serious illness? Has there been a time when you've had to deal with this—in self or others?

Large Group Discussion (20 Minutes)

Facilitator: Ask the people to come together as a large group and facilitate a dialogue on the following questions.

1. What story from your group did you identify with? What did you learn from it?

2. What did you learn or recognize from your experience or from listening to others?

3. Mental, physical, emotional and spiritual health are all important. Do you balance these well or is an area neglected? What skills do you need to become more balanced?

Wrap-up and Evaluation (7–8 Minutes)

Facilitator: Encourage people to talk about how they think the session went. Was everyone involved? Did we contribute to and encourage each other? Announce the theme for next week's session, "Taking Care of My Life." Confirm the details for that session: time, place, date. Who will facilitate, host, and who will bring refreshments? Make sure people remember refreshments are to be simple and easy to serve and eat.

Closing Options (2–4 Minutes)

Facilitator: We recommend you begin this part by asking someone to read one or more of the scripture readings for the following Sunday mass. Later on people may want to do something more. Whatever you do it should be something that all people are comfortable with. There is always the temptation to rush into what I consider the best form of prayer.

Refreshments (1/2 hour)

Facilitator: Make sure that someone has these readily available immediately. (They may be set out in advance.) All the people should be able to eat and socialize easily and leave by the half-hour so that the overall time frame is respected.

YEAR 1 - W - 2

Theme: Taking Care of My Life

Facilitator: Keep in mind the overall time line, but be flexible if the group needs more or less time in any one section. Make sure all ends on time.

Gathering Time—Welcoming and Sharing (15–20 Minutes)

Facilitator: Hospitality should be taking care of itself by now as everyone is co-responsible for it. Have people talk about how they are doing, their day, etc. Keep it brief. Review any parts of the Guidelines for Sharing, pp. 30–31, that you think are important for the group now. Ask someone to do the reflective reading after the focus exercise.

Focus Exercise (2–3 Minutes)

Facilitator: Keep these simple and to the point or select from those on pp. 31–33.

A Reading from *Reader's Digest* article, "To Act or React" by Sidney Harris, July 1960

I walked with my friend, a Quaker, to the news stand the other night, and he bought a paper, thanking the newsie politely. The newsie didn't even acknowledge it.

"A sullen fellow, isn't he," I commented.

"Oh, he's that way every night," shrugged my friend.

"Then why do you continue to be so polite to him?" I asked.

"Why not?" inquired my friend. "Why should I let him decide how I'm going to act?"

As I thought about this incident later, it occurred to me that the important word was "act." My friend acts toward people; most of us react toward them.

He has a sense of inner balance which is lacking in most of us; he knows who he is, what he stands for, how he should behave. He refuses to return incivility for incivility, because then he would no longer be in command of his conduct.

When we are enjoined in the Bible to return good for evil, we look upon this as a moral injunction—which it is. But it is also a psychological prescription for our emotional health.

Nobody is unhappier than the perpetual reactor. His center of emotional gravity is not rooted within himself, where it belongs, but in the world outside him. His spiritual temperature is always being raised or lowered by the social climate around him.

A serenity of spirit cannot be achieved until we become the masters of our own actions and attitudes. (Brief Pause)

A Reading from Philippians 1:6

I am sure of this much: that [God] who has begun the good work in you will carry it through to completion, right up to the day of Christ Jesus.

(Pause for a few moments of reflection)

Small Group Discussion (30 Minutes)

Facilitator: Ask the people to gather in groups of three and dialogue about the following questions. Give them a couple of minutes warning when they have to finish their conversation.

1. Do you recognize who you are? What do you say about who you are?
2. How do you try to be someone else?
3. When are you tempted to lie—or stretch the truth?
4. Do you express your wants and needs or do you expect others to be mind readers? Tell of a time you experienced one or the other.
5. Do you express yourself or suppress yourself? When and where?

Large Group Discussion (20 Minutes)

Facilitator: Ask the people to come together into one large group and facilitate a dialogue about the following questions.

1. What story from your group did you identify with? What did you learn from it?
2. What did you learn or recognize from

your experience or from listening to others?

3. Can you tell a story of someone you admire who is very open about expressing her or his needs?

Wrap-up and Evaluation (5–7 Minutes)

Facilitator: How did we do? Any suggestions? Any final comments or question as we finish? Announce the theme for next session, "Caring for Self and Others." Confirm all the details for next meeting: time, place, directions. Who will facilitate, host, bring refreshments?

Closing Options (2–4 Minutes)

Facilitator: We suggest someone read one or more of the coming Sunday mass readings. This is an important practice for preparation for the Sunday liturgy. If they are heard now in the small group they will be more appreciated and reflected upon on the Sunday. There are other prayer options, pp. 27–30. Whatever you do make sure that everyone will feel comfortable. Deeper prayer times will come after the group has grown together over time, so don't rush it.

Refreshments (1/2 hour)

Enjoy them and socialize. This is an important time but should not be allowed to distract people from departing on time.

YEAR 1 - W - 3

Theme: Caring for Self and Others

Gathering Time—Welcoming and Sharing (15–20 Minutes)

Facilitator: Make sure the welcoming and hospitality go well. Have people talk about their day. Keep all this brief but comfortable. Announce the theme for the session. Briefly review some point or points of the Guidelines for Sharing, pp. 30–31, that may help the group. Ask someone to read the reflective readings after the focus exercise.

Focus Exercise (2–4 Minutes)

Facilitator: There are selections on pp. 31–33.

A Reading by Helen Keller from *Let's Pray 2!* by Br. Charles Reutemann, F.S.C.

Most of us take life for granted. Only the deaf appreciate hearing; only the blind realize the manifold blessings that lie in sight. It is the same old story of not being grateful for what we have until we lose it; of not being conscious of health until we are ill. But I, who am blind, can give one hint to those who see: use your eyes as if tomorrow you would be stricken.

And the same method can be applied to the other senses; hear the music of voices, the song of the bird, the mighty strains of an orchestra, as if you would be stricken deaf tomorrow. Touch each object you want to touch as if tomorrow your tactile sense would fail. Smell the perfume of flowers, taste with relish each morsel, as if tomorrow you could never smell and taste again. Make every sense glory in the facets of the pleasure and beauty which the world reveals. Thus, at last, you will really see, and a new world of beauty will open up before you. (Brief Pause)

A Reading from John 4:13–14

Jesus replied: "Everyone who drinks this water will be thirsty again. But whoever drinks the water I give him will never be thirsty; no, the water I give shall become a fountain within him leaping up to provide eternal life."
(Pause for a few moments of reflection)

Small Group Discussion (20 Minutes)

Facilitator: Ask the people to form groups of three or two and dialogue about the following questions. Remind them that a few moments for reflection on the questions as they begin is good. Also give people a couple of minutes warning to finish their conversations.

1. What do you do to treat yourself well?
2. How do you recognize and handle stress in yourself? How do you create stress for yourself and others?
3. Do you compliment others or complain about others?
4. Do you compliment yourself or put yourself down?
5. When have you asked for help, physically, spiritually, emotionally?
6. Do you volunteer to help others, within the family, at school or work, in the parish, in the community?

Large Group Discussion (30 Minutes)

Facilitator: Ask people to gather again into one large group and dialogue about the following questions.

1. What new ideas on caring for ourselves and others came out of your discussions?
2. Is there a difference in the stress you experience at work, in the family, with friends, peers, church? Do you respond differently?
3. Do you have people you trust to talk with on a spiritual, physical or emotional level? Would you trust the same person in all three areas?

Wrap-up and Evaluation (8–10 Minutes)

Facilitator: Get people discussing how we did at listening to one another. Was it active or passive listening? Are there any other areas that someone would like to comment or ask about? Announce the theme for next week's session, "You Can Lead a Horse to Water…." Confirm the details for the next meeting: time, place, date. Who will facilitate, host, bring refreshments?

Closing Options (2–4 Minutes)

Facilitator: We strongly suggest reading one or more of next Sunday's scripture readings from mass.

Refreshments (1/2 hour)

Enjoy them, the simpler the better. Socialize and finish on time.

YEAR 1 - W - 4

Theme: You Can Lead a Horse to Water….

Gathering Time—Welcoming and Sharing (15–20 Minutes)

Facilitator: By now hospitality should be routine, as well as the socializing and sharing of personal stories. Announce the theme for the session. If there have been any problems review that part of the Guidelines for Sharing, pp. 30–31, that might be helpful. Ask someone to do the readings after the focus exercise.

Focus Exercise (2–3 Minutes)

Facilitator: Choose an option from pp. 31–33.

A Reading from *To Teach as Jesus Did* by the National Conference of Bishops cited in *Let's Pray* by Br. Charles Reutemann, F.S.C.

Education is one of the most important ways

by which the Church fulfills its commitment to the dignity of the person and the building of community. Community is central to educational ministry both as a necessary condition and an ardently desired goal. The educational efforts of the Church must therefore be directed to forming persons-in-community; for the education of the individual Christian is important not only to his solitary destiny but also to the destinies of the many communities in which he lives.

The educational mission of the Church is an integrated ministry embracing three interlocking dimensions: the message revealed by God (*didache*) which the Church proclaims; fellowship in the life of the Holy Spirit (*koinonia*); service to the Christian community and the entire human community (*diakonia*). While these three essential elements can be separated for the sake of analysis, they are joined in the one educational ministry. Each educational program or institution under Church sponsorship is obliged to contribute in its own way to the realization of the threefold purpose within the total educational ministry. (Brief Pause)

A Reading from Hebrews 6:1

Let us, then, go beyond the initial teaching about Christ and advance to maturity.

A Reading from 2 Peter 3:18

Grow rather in grace, and in the knowledge of our Lord and Savior Jesus Christ. Glory be to him now and to the day of eternity! Amen. (Pause for a few moments)

Small Group Discussions (35 Minutes)

Facilitator: Ask people to form groups of three and discuss the following questions. Let them know you'll give them a 2–3 minute warning to finish their conversation. Remind people that the point is not to answer the questions but to use them as points for telling personal experiences.

You probably will not get through all the questions.

1. What was your most recent experience in a formal educational effort, e.g., workshop, classes?
2. What was your reaction? Did it change the way you think? Did you feel renewed or energized? Was it relevant to your life?
3. When have you experienced some education effort or workshop, that you judged a waste of time or a failure?
4. Do you read mostly for pleasure/fun or education/knowledge? Explain.
5. When have you had an insight? For example, a time in your life when you said "Aha! now I understand…." How did it come about?
6. What stimulates insight for you, e.g., discussion with a group, taking a walk alone, books?
7. Insights often call us to climb mountains. Where is your "mountain to climb"? What do you need in order to climb it?

Large Group Discussion (25 Minutes)

Facilitator: Ask the people to come together into one large group for a discussion of the following questions.

1. How do you learn best: from hearing, seeing, touching, etc.?
2. After talking in your groups, what were some of the comments on insights, and where they come from, e.g., reading, education, being in a group?
3. What are some of the communities

that you have been a part of, and how did learning take place?

4. Tell about a time you've had an insight. Did you share it with anyone?

5. What other significant comments came out of your groups?

Wrap-up and Evaluation (5–7 Minutes)

Facilitator: How did we do? Is there something you would like to say that you have not had the opportunity to express? Announce the theme for next week, "Valuing Self." Confirm all the details, especially who will host, facilitate, bring refreshments.

Closing Options (2–4 Minutes)

Facilitator: During this year we especially recommend doing readings from the next Sunday's mass readings for this closing.

Refreshments (1/2 hour)

Enjoy, mingle and leave on time.

YEAR 1 - W - 5

Theme: Valuing Self

Gathering Time—Welcoming and Sharing (15–20 Minutes)

Facilitator: The people should all be good at hospitality by now, but you are always the one to "make sure." People will begin to share about their day, recent personal events. This is important but keep it brief. Announce the theme for the evening. Ask for a reader for the first reading and choose *one* of the scripture readings to be read by a second person after the focus exercise.

Focus Exercise (2–3 Minutes)

Facilitator: There are possibilities, pp. 31–33.

A Reading from *How Can I Help?* by Ram Dass and Paul Groman

One day a rabbi, in a frenzy of religious passion, rushed in before the ark, fell to his knees, and started beating his breast, crying, "I'm nobody! I'm nobody!"

The cantor of the synagogue, pressed by this example of spiritual humility, joined the rabbi on his knees. "I'm nobody! I'm nobody!"

The "shamus" (custodian), watching from the corner, couldn't restrain himself, either. He joined the other two on his knees, calling out, "I'm nobody! I'm nobody!"

At which point the rabbi, nudging the cantor with his elbow, pointed at the custodian and said, "Look who thinks he's nobody!"
(Brief Pause)

Facilitator: Remember to choose one of the following that seems to fit the group, time, place.

A Reading from Hebrews 10:35

Do not, then, surrender your confidence; it will have great reward. You need patience to do God's will and receive what God has promised.

A Reading from Philippians 1:6

I am sure of this much; that [God] who has begun the good work in you will carry it through to completion, right up to the day of Christ Jesus.

A Reading from Habakkuk 3:19

GOD, my Lord, is my strength; [God] makes my feet swift as those of hinds and enables me to go upon the heights.
(Pause for a few moments)

Small Group Discussion (25–30 Minutes)

Facilitator: Ask people to form groups of three and discuss the following questions.

Let them know you'll give a 2–3 minute warning when the time is coming to a close. But be flexible; if they are winding down stop early, if they are really talking give a little more time to finish.

1. Do you ever think: "If people really knew me, they wouldn't like me"?
2. Tell of a time when you have felt that other people know you better than you know yourself.
3. Who are your peers who know you and like you?
4. Tell of a time when you used your imagination, for fantasy, play, or to solve problems.
5. Give an example of what you did when you received an unexpected compliment. What did you do when you got an unexpected complaint? How did you react?
6. When have you been assertive in voicing an opinion?

Large Group Discussion (30 Minutes)

Facilitator: Ask the people to regather into one large group and facilitate a dialogue on the following questions. Allow time for each person to speak. Don't be afraid of "silences" to allow them to gather their thoughts. It's OK not to finish all the questions. The point is to get everyone involved in speaking about their experiences and listening to others' experiences.

1. Do we as individuals, shape our self-worth, or is it formed by our environment, family, world around us?
2. Who do you surround yourself with? Are they people who affirm and support your personal growth and feeling of self-worth?

3. Have you ever associated with people who made you feel bad about yourself, and how did you handle it?
4. How assertive are you? How do people react to you in a group when you have a differing opinion and stand by it? Can you present your idea in a way that people *hear* it, or do they tend to "tune you out"?
5. Give an example of your reaction and response to being complimented.
6. Give an example of your reaction and response to receiving a complaint.
7. Do you see a value in developing your imagination?

Wrap-up and Evaluation (5–10 Minutes)

Facilitator: How did we do? Is there anything you would like to say that you haven't had the opportunity to express? Make sure everyone has a chance to speak. Announce the theme for the next week, "Intimacy." Confirm all the details, especially who will host, facilitate, bring refreshments.

Closing Options (2–4 Minutes)

Facilitator: Ask someone to read one or two of the scriptures for the coming Sunday.

Refreshments (1/2 hour)

Enjoy eating and socializing and finish on time.

YEAR 1 - W - 6

Theme: Intimacy

Gathering Time—Welcoming and Sharing (10–25 Minutes)

Facilitator: This part should go very

smoothly by now with minimal attention from you. Ask people to share the happenings of their week. Announce the theme for the session. If reading from the guidelines for sharing would be helpful, do so. Ask someone to do the readings after the focus exercise.

Focus Exercise (2–3 Minutes)

Facilitator: Exercises are on pp. 31–33.

A Reading from *Gift from the Sea* by Anne Morrow Lindbergh cited in *Let's Pray* by Br. Charles Reutemann, F.S.C.

> It is not the desert island nor the stormy wilderness that cuts you off from the people you love. It is the wilderness in the mind, the desert wastes in the heart through which one wanders lost and a stranger. When one is a stranger to oneself then one is estranged from others too. If one is out of touch with oneself, then one cannot touch others too. How often in a large city, shaking hands with my friends, I have felt the wilderness stretching between us. Both of us were wandering in arid wastes, having lost the springs that nourished us—or having found them dry. Only when one is connected to one's own core is one connected to others, I am beginning to discover. (Brief Pause)

A Reading from the Book of Ruth 1:15–17

> Naomi said to Ruth, "See now, she said, your sister-in-law has gone back to her people and to her god. Go back after your sister-in-law."
>
> But Ruth said, "Do not ask me to abandon or forsake you! for wherever you go, I will go, wherever you lodge, I will lodge, your people shall be my people, and your God, my God. Wherever you die I will die, and there I be buried. May the LORD do so and so to me, and more besides, if aught but death separates me from you!" (Pause briefly)

Small Group Discussion (30 Minutes)

Facilitator: Ask people to form groups of 2–3 and talk about the following questions.

1. Tell about someone you talk with; with whom do you share your thoughts, hopes, dreams?

2. What thoughts, images come to mind when you think of being intimate with someone?

3. Tell about a time when you let your own limitations or those of someone else keep you from intimacy.

4. How do you accept the talents of others? Give an example.

5. Do you ever experience jealousy or competition over another person's talents? If so, what has this done to your relationship with this person?

6. How do you accept the limitations and talents in yourself?

Large Group Discussion (30 Minutes)

Facilitator: Ask the people to form one large group and use the following questions to talk about their life experiences.

1. What were some of the things that struck you as you listened to others tell their stories?

2. Did you gain any insights into your own life, relationships, as you shared with others?

3. Do you accept the limitations of others? Have you talked to someone to help them see a shortcoming? Is this your responsibility?

4. How have you reacted when someone has pointed out a limitation that they perceive in you?

5. How do you draw out and celebrate the talents in others?

6. What does it mean to be intimate with someone?

Wrap-up and Evaluation (5–10 Minutes)

Facilitator: How did we do? Is there something someone wants to say? Announce the theme for next session, "Service." Since the next session is the last what shall we do to celebrate? Confirm the details, hosting, facilitating, bringing refreshments.

Closing Options (2–4 Minutes)

Facilitator: Read from the scripture for Sunday.

Refreshments (1/2 hour)

Enjoy.

YEAR 1 - W - 7

Theme: Service

Gathering Time—Welcoming and Sharing (10–15 Minutes)

Facilitator: Make sure all goes well in hospitality and sharing about the events of the day. Announce the theme for the session. Ask someone to do the readings after the focus exercise.

Focus Exercise (2–3 Minutes)

A Reading from *Review for Religious,* "Ministry in the Church: A Structural Concern for Justice" by Francis X. Meehan, Jan. 1978

> Once there was a farming town that could be reached by a narrow road with a bad curve in it. There were frequent accidents on the road especially at the curve, and the preacher would preach to the people of the town to make sure they were Good Samaritans. And so they were, as they would pick the people up on the road, for this was a religious work.

> One day someone suggested they buy an ambulance to get the accident victims to the town hospital more quickly. The preacher preached and the people gave, for this was a religious war. Then one day a councilman suggested that the town authorize building a wider road and taking out the dangerous curve. Now it happened that the mayor had a farm market right at the curve on the road and he was against taking out the curve. Someone asked the preacher to say a word to the mayor and the congregation next Sunday about it. But the preacher and most of the people figured they had better stay out of politics; so the next Sunday the preacher preached on the Good Samaritan Gospel and encouraged the people to continue their fine work of picking up the accident victims— which they did.
> (Brief Pause)

A Reading from 2 Corinthians 9:6–8

> Let me say this much: He who sows sparingly will reap sparingly, and he who sows bountifully will reap bountifully. Everyone must give according to what each has inwardly decided; not sadly, not grudgingly, for God loves a cheerful giver. God can multiply his favors among you so that you may always have enough of everything and even a surplus for good works.
> (Pause for a few moments)

Small Group Discussion (30 Minutes)

Facilitator: Ask the people to break up into groups of three and discuss the following questions. You'll give them a couple of minutes warning to wrap up the conversation.

1. Name some unique gift that you have. Tell a little about how you use it.
2. Tell of a time when you have been of service to:
   —a group
   —the church
   —community or school

Choose one of the above examples of service and talk about how you felt about it, and how others reacted.

3. Have you ever been challenged to do some kind of service that called for a gift you didn't think you had?

4. Do you see your life's work as a vocation or a profession? Why?

5. What form(s) of service do you admire most in others? Is it something you hope to do some day?

6. Name a gift you see in others in this group. Remember that every person has some gift.

Large Group Discussion (30 Minutes)

Facilitator: Ask the people to gather as one group again and facilitate a dialogue about the following questions.

1. What type of service do you admire in others? If you hope to do this type of service some day, what kinds of skills do you need to develop?

2. Name a time when you performed a service for someone. How did you feel? How did the person/persons react?

3. Tell about a time when someone was of service to you. How did you feel? What did you say to the person (people)?

4. Name a gift you see in others in the group. (Make sure everyone is mentioned. Responses can be spontaneous or you can go around the room, person by person.) Encourage people to name "gifts"—not just state "happy" or "friendly"—but e.g., "able to lift up others spirits," or "taking on responsibility."

Wrap-up and Evaluation (10 Minutes)

Facilitator: Since this is the final session of the set make sure that there is a good critique. Someone should take notes. The parish will probably want a report. Ask people to think back over the past weeks and comment on their experiences. This is usually a very important validating session for everyone. Are there any suggestions for the future? Make sure that all the details are taken care of if there is to be a celebration at another time or place, e.g., social outing, or a festive dinner.

Also encourage everyone to be in contact for the beginning of the next set of sessions. If you can fix a date that would be great; if not get everyone's name and phone number to give them a call in plenty of time to get it on their schedule.

Closing Options (4–5 Minutes)

Facilitator: We suggest that in addition to the reading from next Sunday's scripture you might also do a prayer service. There are examples in chapter 3, pp. 27–30 for your modeling or use.

Refreshments (1/2 hour)

Unless a special celebration has been planned and everyone is ready for the extra time, enjoy!

YEAR 1 - S - 1

Theme: Reconnections—Telling Our Story

Facilitator: It is important to focus on hospitality this first session, welcoming people, especially any newcomers to the group. Depending on the response of the group, you may want to allow more or less time for some parts of the process. Always keep in mind the overall timeline, so that you allow time for evaluation and end promptly.

Gathering Time—Welcoming and Sharing (15 Minutes)

Facilitator: Make sure everyone has been introduced and becomes comfortable. Continue to facilitate a sharing of what has happened recently in life since the group last met. It is good to review the Guidelines for Sharing, pp. 30–31, at this time and make sure that everyone has a copy. Also announce the theme, and that interwoven throughout it will be the values of belonging and self-esteem. Ask someone to read the reading after the focus exercise.

Focus Exercise (2–3 Minutes), pp. 31–33.

A Reading from "The Lioness," *The Fables of Aesop*

> A great rivalry existed among the beasts of the forest over which could produce the largest litter. Some shamefacedly admitted having only two, while others boasted proudly of having a dozen.
>
> At last the committee called upon the lioness. "And to how many cubs do you give birth?" they asked the proud lioness.
>
> "One," she replied sternly, "but that *one* is a lion!"
>
> (Pause for a few moments of reflection)

Small Group Discussion (15–20 Minutes)

Facilitator: Ask the group to break up into groups of three. Ask that they take a few minutes to reflect on the questions before discussing. You'll again give them a two-minute signal to wrap up their discussions.

1. Think about two or three highlights that occurred in your life since we met during the last set of sessions. Tell about these events. Who were the people involved and what were your feelings? (As a listener, pay attention to the people involved, your own feelings, and why these experiences are significant.)

2. What was the major liturgical event during the Holy Week/Easter for you? Why?

3. Were there any similarities/connections in the stories that were told?

Large Group Discussion (30 Minutes)

Facilitator: Ask people to gather again and continue by discussing the following questions.

1. What story from your group did you identify with? What did you learn from it?

2. What did you learn or recognize from your experience or from listening to others?

3. As a group, summarize some physical actions and words that are signs of caring, valuing, showing interest and concern. In what groups are you comfortable using these actions, words? In what groups wouldn't you use them?

Wrap-up and Evaluation (5 Minutes)

Facilitator: Encourage people to talk about how they thought the evening went. Was everyone involved. Did we encourage each other? Announce the theme for next week, "Play and Fantasy." Confirm the details for next meeting. Who facilitates, hosts, brings refreshments?

Closing Options: (2–4 Minutes)

Facilitator: We recommend reading a scripture passage from the following Sunday liturgy, especially the gospel. You may also have a short structured prayer service as suggested on pp. 27–30. By this time we would hope that prayer or scripture reading would have been begun to be regularly done for closing.

Refreshments: (1/2 hour)

Facilitator: Remember to make sure people enjoy eating and socializing, but keep to the time frame so that people can get on with their busy lives.

YEAR 1 - S - 2

Theme: Recreation—Play and Fantasy

Facilitator: It is important that you keep in mind the overall time frame, but be flexible if the group needs more or less time in any one section. Be sure to begin and end on time.

Gathering Time—Welcoming and Sharing (10–15 Minutes)

Facilitator: Take the first few minutes to get people talking about how they are doing, how their time has been. This refocusing into the group is important. Announce the theme for the session. Make some comment about the Guidelines for Sharing, pp. 30–31, maybe highlighting something you think is important. Ask for someone to do the reading after the focus exercise.

Focus Exercise (2–3 Minutes), pp. 31–33.

A Reading from *St. George and the Dragon* by Edward Hays

God had taken the day off and was lounging in a large, green canvas lawn chair in the center of creation. Clustered around God were several archangels, and together they were admiring what had been accomplished in only six short days. Paradise was alive with activity as birds of all colors and shapes flew from tree to tree, filling the air with a multitude of marvelous melodies. Creatures of all sizes and descriptions moved gracefully among the clusters of wildflowers heavy with blossoms.

God sipped a tall, frosted glass of lemonade, looked out over all that had been created and said, "Hmmm, that's good…but, it could be better!"

"I think I should change just a few things here and there; it just doesn't look right. Something's missing."

"You've hit upon it, Michael," said God, alive with excitement. "That's the problem: it's just too orderly. There's no spontaneity! You don't get any sense of energy. What's missing is the dynamic element. Take Adam, for example. Look at him over there. See what I mean?"

The very next day God appeared at the weekly staff meeting, and with delight dancing on every word, announced, "I have solved my problem. And it is also theoretically possible even if I am a bit hesitant because of the potential danger involved." "What I am proposing…, is to split my Adam!"

A gasp of disbelief escaped from the shocked angels. Raphael said, "O my God, think of the consequences: radiation, nuclear winds, fire storms, mutations and untold cosmic disturbances!"

"Nope, my mind is made up. If you aren't ready to risk, you'll never taste life, and nothing creative or beautiful will ever happen. I'm taking the risk; tomorrow morning we will attempt to split the Adam."

In the purple pre-dawn darkness, as Adam dreamed away in a deep sleep, the

Lord God knelt over him with an upraised silver hammer. Like a master jeweler poised over a goose-sized diamond, the Lord God hovered over Adam, calculating at what precise angle and speed the blow should fall.

Adam's cry of separation seared the pre-dawn silence, and the roar was deafening. As a massive orange-red fireball ballooned skyward, God looked down on the split Adam and saw...the beloved Adam, was now not one but two.

The Archangel Michael, hanging on with both hands to the great Tree of Life in the center of the garden, shouted over the deafening roar, "And, Lord God, what shall we call this newest creation—this electrifying energy?"

"I think," God shouted back, white hair streaming in the wind, face beaming with the sweet smile of success, "I think I'll call it LOVE."

(Pause for a few moments of reflection)

Large Group Discussion (30 Minutes)

Facilitator: Ask people to break into groups of three and talk about the following questions.

1. What do you do for recreation? What is your favorite recreation?
2. When have you ever been spontaneous, undirected? Describe one experience, and tell how you felt about it.
3. Do you ever turn your imagination loose? Think of a time when this happened. Was it a fun experience? Did you feel guilty about "wasting time"?
4. Can the use of imagination be energizing, a source of pleasure? Share and talk about this.
5. When have you experienced fantasy? How did it make you feel?
6. Are recreation/play/fantasy important for you? Do you feel you have a balance of these vs. "work"? Is it something you could/should do more often?

Large Group Discussion (30 Minutes)

Facilitator: Ask the groups to come back together and discuss the following questions. Explain that sometimes in the large group we ask the same questions that have just been discussed in the small groups. The idea is to help one another expand on telling our own story. The more we tell our story, and the more people give feedback the more we come to awareness about the events and episodes of our life.

1. What do you do for recreation? How do you feel when you take the time to recreate? Do you think you give yourself enough time for this?
2. Is spontaneity part of your life or is everything orderly? If you experience spontaneity, does it make you feel energized and dynamic?
3. Is there a place for fantasy in your life? Are you a person who fantasizes well? Does it take special timing, skill and risk to fantasize?
4. What did you hear or say in your small group that you think is valuable for all of us to hear?

Wrap-up and Evaluation: (5 Minutes)

Facilitator: How did the session go? Any suggestions? Any final comments?

Announce the theme for next week, "Revisiting Where We've Been." Confirm the details for next session. Who will facilitate, host, bring refreshments?

Closing Option: (2–4 Minutes)

Refreshments: (1/2 hour)

YEAR 1 - S - 3

Theme: Revisiting Where We've Been

Gathering—Welcoming and Sharing (10–15 Minutes)

Facilitator: Hospitality should be happening easily by now. Help get people seated and take a few minutes to visit and share the latest events. Keep all this brief. If you think it necessary mention something about the Guidelines for Sharing. Announce the theme for the session and ask for someone to read the reflection after the focus exercise.

Focus Exercise (2–3 Minutes)

A Reading from *Stations of the Cross* by Parker Palmer

A great naturalist once spent time in a seaside town called Costabel and, plagued by his life-long insomnia, spent the early morning hours walking the beach. Each day at sunrise he found townspeople combing the sand for starfish which had washed ashore during the night, to kill them for commercial purposes. It was, for Eiseley, a sign, however small, of all the ways the world says no to life.

But one morning Eiseley got up unusually early, and discovered a solitary figure on the beach. This man, too, was gathering starfish, but each time he found one alive he would pick it up and throw it as far as he could out beyond the breaking surf, back to the nurturing ocean from which it came. As days went by Eiseley found this man embarked on his mission of mercy each morning, seven days a week, no matter the weather.

Eiseley named this man "the star thrower," and in a moving meditation he writes of how this man and his predawn work contradicted everything that Eiseley had been taught about evolution and the survival of the fittest. Here on the beach in Costabel the strong reached down to save, not crush, the weak.

And Eiseley wonders: Is there a star thrower at work in the universe, a God who contradicts death, a God whose nature (in the words of Thomas Merton) is "mercy within mercy within mercy"?
(Pause for a few moments of reflection)

Large Group Discussion (10–15 Minutes)

Facilitator: Ask the group to discuss the following questions.

1. Talk about the sessions from the last two weeks or last quarter. Name the themes of each week (Reconnections—Telling my Story—Recreation; Play and Fantasy). In our time together, think back and reflect about what has happened. What are some of the things you have learned? Has there been growth? How was it experienced?

Small Group Discussion (30 Minutes)

Facilitator: Ask people to break up into groups of three. Remind them to reflect on the questions before beginning the discussion. Give them a two minute signal to finish discussing.

1. Who sustains and supports you in good times and difficult times? Tell of an experience of being supported in each type of situation.

2. Tell of a time when you've been part of a group which supported someone else in good times and difficult times. How did that seem or feel to you?

3. Has your experience of sharing thoughts and emotions with others changed over the past few weeks? Can you give an example?

Large Group Discussion (20–25 Minutes)

Facilitator: Regather the groups and ask someone to read the following scripture. Pause briefly and then begin a general discussion of the questions.

A Reading from Matthew 12:46–50

He was still addressing the crowds when his mother and his brothers appeared outside to speak with him. Someone said to him, "Your mother and your brothers are standing out there and they wish to speak to you."

He said to the one who had told him, "Who is my mother? Who are my brothers?" Then, extending his hand toward his disciples, he said, "There are my mother and my brothers. Whoever does the will of my heavenly Father is brother and sister and mother to me."

(Pause for a moment of reflection)

1. Briefly, what does scripture say about our discussion and experience?

2. Your family is your first partner on your faith journey. Have you added companions on your faith journey? Who are they? Have some companions changed, increased or continued?

3. Where are you in sharing your faith journey?

Wrap-up and Evaluation (3–5 Minutes)

Facilitator: Are there any other comments that need to be made? Announce that the theme for next week will be "Community Support." Cover the details for the next meeting. Who facilitates, hosts, brings refreshments?

Closing Options: (2–4 Minutes)

Refreshments: (1/2 hour)

YEAR 1 - S - 4

Theme: Community Support

Gathering Time—Welcoming and Sharing (10–15 Minutes)

Facilitator: Make sure that good greeting and hospitality is happening. Make sure that people are seated and comfortably sharing about what's been going on. Keep it brief. Announce the theme for the session and ask for someone to read the reflection after the focus exercise.

Focus Exercise (2–3 Minutes)

A Reading from "The Traveler and the Hatchet," *The Fables of Aesop*

Two men were traveling along the highroad toward the town. Suddenly one of them spied a hatchet half hidden in the fallen leaves.

"Look what I have found!" he cried, picking up the tool.

"Do not say 'I,' " replied his companion. "It is more proper to say, 'Look what *we* have found!' "

The finder of the hatchet shrugged his shoulders, and they continued on their way. Presently they came upon a group of men whose eyes were on the roadway as though they were looking for something. Suddenly one of the strangers pointed to the approaching couple, and they rushed up to them, pointing to the hatchet.

"Alas," said the traveler who had found the hatchet, "it looks as though we are in trouble."

"What do you mean *'we* are in trouble'? What you really mean to say is that 'I am in trouble!'"

(Pause for few moments of silence)

Small Group Discussion (30 Minutes)

Facilitator: Ask people to divide into groups of three and discuss the following questions. You will give them a two-minute signal to finish their discussions.

1. When have you promoted cooperation between individuals?

2. When have you promoted cooperation between groups of people, e.g., between neighbors, families, departments, committees (church, business, civic), organizations?

3. Where have you experienced different people who aid and add to each other by thoughts and actions? Describe a situation.

4. Where and how have others helped you? How do you feel when this happens?

5. Has there been a time when you went to other people with different skills, talents, viewpoints, to cooperate for a common task or experience? Can you describe this and how it happened?

6. How many people know you well? Do these people know each other?

Large Group Discussion (30 Minutes)

Facilitator: Regather the large group and ask them to discuss the following questions.

1. When you have a party, who do you invite?

2. How many people know you well? Do they know each other?

3. Where and how have others helped you? How do you feel when this happens?

4. Are you learning more skills for accepting and receiving mutual support? Do you have an example to tell?

5. Was there something said in your

small group that gives you insight into something in your own life?

Wrap-up and Evaluation (5 Minutes)

Facilitator: Is there anything else that needs to be said, or that you want to express? Announce the theme for next week, "Listening—Insight." Go over details for next session. Who hosts, facilitates, brings refreshments?

Closing Options (2–4 Minutes)

Refreshments (1/2 hour)

Enjoy!

YEAR 1 - S - 5

Theme: Listening—Insight

Gathering Time—Welcoming and Sharing (10–15 Minutes)

Facilitator: Remember that all the members of the group are co-responsible for hospitality and sharing. This should be happening regularly. You are particularly responsible to the whole group for the time frame. So begin and end with the time allotted. Announce the topic and ask someone to read the reflection after the focus exercise.

Focus Exercise (2–3 Minutes)

A Reading from "The Three Tradesmen," *The Fables of Aesop*

> The enemy stood outside the walls of a certain city. As they brought up their siege weapons and they arranged their forces for the attack, the desperate defenders within held a council of war to determine the best means of holding their city.

A bricklayer arose. "Sirs," said he, "it is my opinion that the best material for this purpose is brick." Then he sat down.

A carpenter asked to be recognized. "I beg to differ with the bricklayer. The material that will best serve our desperate needs is wood. Let timber be our defense!"

Then a tanner jumped to his feet. "Citizens," he cried, "when you all have had your say, I wish to remind you that there is nothing in the world like leather!"

(Pause for a few moments of reflection)

Small Group Discussion (30 Minutes)

Facilitator: Ask people to form groups of three and talk about the following questions. Let the groups know the time frame and that you'll give a signal for wrap-up two minutes before the end.

1. Tell of an experience when you were a good listener.
2. Have you improved in listening skills this year? Can you give an example?
3. What have you gained from listening? How did you feel during and after you really listened to someone?
4. When you were really present and listening to someone, what happened to the person who was talking? Were you aware of their reaction to you?
5. What insights have you experienced from really listening to people? Has this carried over to your everyday life?
6. Insights are spontaneous/intuitive. In the past, where have you experienced them? Therefore, where would you likely expect them in the future?

Large Group Discussion (30 Minutes)

Facilitator: Regather the large group and facilitate a dialogue about the following questions.

1. Share a story from your small group of an example of good listening.
2. Do you think that you are normally an intuitive person? Can you think of a time when you were not sensitive to someone as they were talking, and the effect on them?
3. Who are some of the intuitive people that you know? What can you learn from them?
4. Thinking back to the first reading, who in the story was thinking of the common good of the people? Have you had a similar kind of experience?
5. What skills do you need to develop in order to hear everyone's idea? Reflect back to the group the common theme expressed by all.

Wrap-up and Evaluation (5 Minutes)

Facilitator: Is there anything else that needs to be said? The theme for next week is "What's Good News for You." Confirm details about next week. Who facilitates, hosts, brings refreshments?

Closing Options (2–4 Minutes)

Refreshments (1/2 hour)

YEAR 1 - S - 6

Theme: What's Good News for You

Gathering Time—Welcoming and Sharing (10–15 Minutes)

Facilitator: Let the gathering hospitality go on for a short time encouraging all to talk. Announce the theme for the session. Ask someone to do the reading after the focus exercise.

Focus Exercise (2–3 Minutes)

A Reading from Mark 1:29–39

> Immediately upon leaving the synagogue, he entered the house of Simon and Andrew with James and John. Simon's mother-in-law lay ill with a fever, and the first thing they did was to tell him about her. He went over to her and grasped her hand and helped her up, and the fever left her. She immediately began to wait on them.
>
> After sunset, as evening drew on, they brought him all who were ill, and those possessed by demons. Before long the whole town was gathered outside the door. Those whom he cured, who were variously afflicted, were many, and so were the demons he expelled. But he would not permit the demons to speak, because they knew him. Rising early the next morning, he went off to a lonely place in the desert; there he was absorbed in prayer. Simon and his companions managed to track him down, and when they found him, they told him, "Everybody is looking for you!" He said to them: "Let us move on to the neighboring villages so that I may proclaim the good news there also." So he went into their synagogues preaching the good news and expelling demons throughout the whole of Galilee.

(Pause for a few moments of reflection)

Small Group Discussion (30 Minutes)

Facilitator: Ask people to form groups of three and discuss the following questions.

1. When have you experienced good news? How?
2. What has been the "best" news for you this year? How did you receive it?
3. Do you see other people's personal stories as good news? How can you

become better at telling your stories, and making a connection with the good news?
4. What are the events and happenings that occurred to you this year that created good news in your life? (Not necessarily all happy events)
5. What's the gospel been for you this year?

Large Group Discussion (30 Minutes)

Facilitator: Ask the people to form a large group. Reread the scripture passage and then facilitate a discussion on the following questions.

1. What has been the best news for you this year?
2. Did any word or thought from the scripture reading strike you in particular as you listened to the gospel? What comments do you have about it?
3. What good news did you hear in the other person's story?
4. Did anything that you heard here make you reevaluate what is good news for you?

Wrap-up and Evaluation (5–10 Minutes)

Facilitator: Is there anything that needs to be said, other comments? The theme of next week will be "Looking Back and Looking Forward." As you can tell, that will be the last session until the fall. Do we want to have a special celebration? How? When? The details of this need to be worked out now. Also, who will facilitate next week's session, who will host, and who bring refreshments?

Closing Option (2–4 Minutes)

Refreshments (1/2 hour)

Enjoy and socialize.

YEAR 1 - S - 7

Theme: Looking Back and Looking Forward

Facilitator: This is the closing session for this set and for this year. The time frame is tighter then normal, so please be aware of the times suggested. This closing session is divided into three sections: Evaluation, Small Group/Large Group Sharing and Closing. This is arranged to get the more practical items completed first. However, if people would like to add more notes to the evaluation after the closing, please encourage them to do so.

Gathering Time—Welcoming and Sharing (10 Minutes)

Facilitator: Please gather people in order to begin on time, and announce the theme.

Evaluation (15 Minutes)

Facilitator: The parish will probably want a short year-end report, so please ask someone to record the comments. (We recommend using newsprint so that everyone can see the comments as they are added. It can be typed later). Additional personal comments may be added later. If the parish is having an end of the year gathering, announce it, and provide a handout with details, if the parish has not already done that.

Questions:

1. How has this group and process been helpful to us as individuals and as a group?

2. Do you see that this experience in a small group might have a long-lasting or even permanent effect on your life? In what way?

3. What skills do you need, to continue to develop as a whole person?

Facilitator: Make sure that all the notes (hopefully newsprint) are collected. Remind people that they can add more personal things at the end, and then ask people to continue the session with a reflection. Who will read?

A Reading from *I Begin to See* by Thomas M. Corry

> When I was six
> I loved looking at myself in the mirror
> At 16 I hated it—and continued to do so until
> I was 49
> except sometimes recently.
>
> What I am never seemed to match
> what I *saw* reflected back at me.
> Sometimes I am shocked
> at what I think I feel I am
> compared to what I think I see.
>
> Mirrors don't reveal me to me
> but people do—Reflecting
> my magic in ways that I
> never imagined possible
> and I like what I see.
> (Pause for a few moments of reflection)

Small Group Discussion (20 Minutes)

Facilitator: Please explain that for question #4, each person is asked to reflect about one other person in the group, how they saw this person when they first met, and how they appreciate her/him now. Be sure the instructions are clear. Ask the people to break into groups of three and talk about the following questions.

1. What is the most memorable thing that happened in our small group?
2. Have we, as a group, changed in our time together?
3. Have you as an individual changed in our time together?
4. Choose a person in the group and say what you most appreciate about this person, and why.

Large Group Discussion (20 Minutes)

Facilitator: Ask people to regather and discuss the following. It is important here to make sure that each person gets an appreciation mention.

1. Introduce the person you spoke about in your small group to the large group, saying what it is you appreciate about him/her and why. (After a person has finished others in the group can add any comments they wish to make.)

Closing Options (10–15 Minutes)

Tonight it might be appropriate to have a reading from the Sunday scripture plus a short prayer service. This needs to have been planned ahead. Make sure everyone gets to participate.

Refreshments (1/2 hour)

Enjoy and socialize.

CHAPTER 5

YEAR 2 - F - 1

Theme: Renew, Review, Revisit

Facilitator: Make sure that everyone feels welcomed back to the group. Focus on hospitality; especially for any newcomers, from the initial greeting at the door to departure. New people may feel more comfortable sharing with a couple of people rather than the large group. You need to encourage participation without making them feel guilty. Explain that by not sharing, they deprive the whole group of possibly another point of view. Ask people to mull over the issue—what does it mean in their life, what other questions does it raise—and then to share their thoughts, feelings and experiences.

Gathering Time—Welcoming and Sharing (10–15 Minutes)

Facilitator: Welcome everyone and thank them for being there. Make sure every person is introduced or reintroduced. This might include saying something briefly about some personal incident over the summer. Announce the theme for the session and remind people of the general outline of the time together (small groups for questions, large group with more questions and closing with refreshments). Make sure everyone has a copy of the Guidelines for Sharing, pp. 30–31, and review quickly. Ask someone to read the reading for reflection after the focus exercise.

Focus Exercise (2–3 Minutes) (Options pp. 31–33)

A Reading from *Seeds of Contemplation,* by Thomas Merton

> Sooner or later, if we follow Christ, we have to risk everything in order to gain everything....cowardice keeps us "double-minded"—hesitating between the world and God. In this hesitating there is no true faith—faith remains an opinion. We are never certain, because we never quite give in to the authority of an invisible God.
> (Pause for a few moments of reflection)

Small Group Discussion (20 Minutes)

Facilitator: Ask people to break up into groups of three, two if necessary, and talk about the following. Ask people to read through all the questions before beginning the discussion. Tell them how much time they will have, and that you will give them a two-minute wrap-up signal. Each group is reminded to allow each person time to speak. Monitor how the small groups are doing. If they need a few more minutes, or seem to be ready a few minutes early, adjust the schedule accordingly.

1. What has been happening in your life since the group last met?
2. What insights or understanding do you have about yourself after being a part of this group this past year?

3. What insights or understanding do you have about others after your participation in the group this past year?

4. How are you involved in the Communion of Saints/Community of the Faithful? Tell what you are doing.

Large Group Discussion (40 Minutes)

Facilitator: Ask the people to regather into the large group and dialogue about the following.

1. Tell a story of something that happened to you over the summer.

2. In what ways are you involved in the institutional structure of the family, church, school, community?

3. Over the summer have you rethought your involvement with any of these structures? Do you feel a stronger commitment now than you did in the beginning? Does it challenge you to grow? If so, how?

Wrap-up and Evaluation (5–10 Minutes)

Facilitator: Encourage everyone to talk about how this first session went. Did everyone feel comfortable, welcomed? Did you take the risk of being really involved? Announce the theme for next week, "Sensual Pleasure—Individual and Communal."

Confirm the details for next time.

Who will host the next session? Get directions if needed.

Who will provide refreshments the next time?

Who will facilitate? Remind them everyone is to take a turn.

Closing Option: (2–4 Minutes)

We suggest that one or more of the scripture readings for the following Sunday be read to close each session during this set. The reading is for hearing in silence.

Refreshments: (1/2 hour)

Remember to have simple refreshments and have them ready to serve so that everyone can socialize and enjoy, but end with the time framework.

YEAR 2 - F - 2

Theme: Sensual Pleasure—Individual and Communal

Gathering Time: Welcoming and Sharing (15 Minutes)

Facilitator: Make sure that welcoming and hospitality go well. Ask everyone to take a few minutes to talk about their past week, and how their day has been. Make sure all have a chance to speak. Announce the theme. We suggest that you review one part of the Guidelines for Sharing, pp. 30–31. Ask someone to read the reflection after the focus exercise.

Focus Exercise (2–3 Minutes), pp. 31–33.

A Reading from "Give Me Ears to Hear," *Guerrillas of Grace* **by Ted Loder**

Lord,
I believe
    my life is touched by you,
        that you want something for me,
            and of me.
Give me ears
    to hear you,
eyes
    to see the tracing of your finger,
and a heart
        quickened by the motions
        of your Spirit.
(Pause for a few moments of reflection)

Small Group Discussion (20 Minutes)

Facilitator: Ask people to break up into groups of three for the following discussion questions.

1. To whom do you belong? Tell a story that will illustrate this.
2. How do you feel and/or think about our parish? Are these feelings and/or thoughts based on what you *do* or just by *being* a member?
3. What senses are activated by your attending this parish?
4. We each have five senses: sight, hearing, smell, touch and taste. What is one experience of sensual pleasure in parish life that you can relate; e.g., within liturgy, a social event, or something involving the poor?

Large Group Discussion (40 Minutes)

Facilitator: Regather the whole group and facilitate a dialogue about the following questions.

1. How do you feel and/or think that you are important to your parish?
2. What is one experience of sensual pleasure in parish life that you can relate; e.g., within liturgy, a social event, or something involving the poor?
3. Tell a story of a time when you only responded to others in the parish on a thinking level. Now tell of a time when you related to others on a feeling/sensual level, for example, spending time on hospitality, greeting, making people feel welcome.

Wrap-up and Evaluation (5 Minutes)

Facilitator: Ask how people did in listening actively to one another. How do you feel we are doing at making people feel important? Announce the theme for the next session, "Equality." Confirm the next meeting date and details.

Who will host the next session? Get directions if needed.

Who will provide refreshments the next time?

Who will facilitate? Remind them everyone is to take a turn.

Closing Options (2–4 Minutes)

Facilitator: Read one or more of next Sunday's scriptures.

Refreshments (1/2 hour)

Keep refreshments simple and ready to serve.

YEAR 2 - F - 3

Theme: Equality

Gathering Time—Welcoming and Sharing (8–10 Minutes)

Facilitator: Everyone should be getting into the welcoming activity. You are to keep the time frame. Help people to be seated and talk about how their days have gone. Make sure everyone gets involved. This is to help the gathering process. Announce the theme. Again review something from the Guidelines for Sharing, something that you think is important for the group. Ask for someone to read after the focus exercise.

Focus Exercise (2–3 Minutes)

A Reading from the Inscription on the Statue of Liberty

Give me your tired, your poor, your huddled masses yearning to be free, the wretched refuse of your teeming shore. Send these, the homeless, tempest tossed to me. I lift my lamp beside the golden door.
(Pause for a few moments of silence and reflection)

Small Group Discussion (25 Minutes)

Facilitator: Ask the people to break up into groups of three. Give them a two-minute signal before ending, to allow time to finish their discussion of the following questions.

1. How do you relate to other generations, race, gender? Give an example.
2. When have you practiced equality or inequality with a person of another generation or a person of the opposite sex, someone whose life choices you don't agree with? To what was it due?
3. When you have felt equal with another? To what was it due?
4. Tell a story about when you felt unequal with another, how did it make you feel?
5. Do you feel free to express your feelings and ideas in groups? Give an example.

Large Group Discussion (35 Minutes)

Facilitator: Regather the groups into one large group and facilitate a discussion of the following questions.

1. When you have felt equal with another person, was it because of something they did, or something you did?
2. When you experienced inequality with another, how did you feel?
3. What skills do you need to develop to be able to express yourself with equality through all your actions?

Wrap-up and Evaluation (10 Minutes)

Facilitator: Did you feel free to express your ideas today? What helped you to do this? What hindered this happening? Announce the theme for the next session, "Expectations." Confirm the next meeting date and details.

Who will host—provide refreshments—who will facilitate?

Closing Option (2–4 Minutes)

Facilitator: Read next Sunday's scriptures.

Refreshments (1/2 hour)

Have refreshments ready to serve immediately, so the group can socialize and leave within a half-hour.

YEAR 2 - F - 4

Theme: Expectations
Allowing Others to Decide the Rules

Gathering time—Welcoming and Sharing (10 Minutes)

Facilitator: Welcome and hospitality should be easy for all members of the group to practice by now. Make sure everyone is taking time to tell how they are doing, to get settled down and comfortable. Announce the theme for the session. If you think it is needed remind everyone of some part of the Guidelines for Sharing. Ask someone to do the reading after the focus exercise.

Focus Exercise (2–3 Minutes)

A Reading from *Seeds of Contemplation* **by Thomas Merton**

> Living is not thinking. Thought is formed and guided by…reality outside us. Living is the constant adjustment of thought to life and life to thought in such a way that we are always growing, always experiencing new things in the old and old things in the new. This life is always new.
>
> (Pause for a few moments of reflection)

Small Group Discussion (25 Minutes)

Facilitator: Ask the people to form into groups of two or three and talk about the following questions.

1. Give an example of an expectation you have of yourself.
2. How do you deal with failing to live up to your expectations for yourself?
3. Do you feel you live your life by other people's rules without thinking about it?
4. Do you ever question the rules?

Large Group Discussion (35 Minutes)

Facilitator: Regather the large group and lead a dialogue about these questions.

1. Give an example of an expectation someone important to you has for you.
2. What have you learned from your failures at living up to your own expectations?
3. Is this type of learning as valuable as what you learn from successes? In what way?
4. Can you tell a story of a time when you recognized that other people's rules weren't for you.

Wrap-up and Evaluation (5–7 Minutes)

Facilitator: How do you see these small parish groups as a way of learning, as having an impact on your life and how you live it? Do your expectations for the group get in the way with your being open and honest in your sharing? Announce the theme for the next session, "Incarnation—Enfleshment."

Inform people that in two weeks there will be a partial "do-it-yourself" session written by the group out of your own experiences. Confirm details for the next session. Who will host, facilitate, bring refreshments?

Closing Options (2–4 Minutes)

Read some of next Sunday's scriptures.

Refreshments (1/2 hour)

YEAR 2 - F - 5

Theme: Incarnation—Enfleshment

Gathering Time—Welcoming and Sharing (10 Minutes)

Facilitator: Make sure welcoming and hospitality works. Make sure everyone takes time to talk and get comfortable. Announce the theme for this session. Ask someone to read after the focus exercise.

Focus Exercise (2–3 Minutes)

A Reading from *Seeds of Contemplation* **by Thomas Merton**

> There is no greater disaster in the spiritual life than to be immersed in unreality, for life is maintained and nourished in us by our united relation with realities outside and above us. When life feeds on unreality, it must starve.
>
> (Pause)

A Reading from Matthew 1:18–24

Now this is how the birth of Jesus Christ came about. When his mother Mary was engaged to Joseph, but before they lived together, she was found with child through the power of the Holy Spirit. Joseph her husband, an upright man unwilling to expose her to the law, decided to divorce her quietly. Such was his intention when suddenly the angel of the Lord appeared in a dream and said to him: "Joseph, son of David, have no fear about taking Mary as your wife. It is by the Holy Spirit that she has conceived this child. She is to have a son and you are to name him Jesus because he will save his people from their sins." All this happened to fulfill what the Lord had said through the prophet: "The virgin shall be with child and give birth to a son, and they shall call him Emmanuel," a name which means "God is with us." When Joseph awoke he did as the angel of the Lord had directed him and received her into his home as his wife. He had no relations with her at any time before she bore a son, whom he named Jesus.
(Pause for reflection)

Small Group Discussion (25 Minutes)

Facilitator: Ask the people to break into groups of three for the following dialogue.

1. Tell a story of a past Christmas tradition you've had.
2. Name some of the people and relate some of the events that make God real to you in your life.
3. Matthew 1:23: "The Virgin shall be with child and give birth to a son, and they shall call him Emmanuel," a name which means "God-is-with-us." Do you experience this event as something that happened 2000 years ago, or do you feel that it happens in your daily life?

4. How have you helped to make this event believable to yourself and others? Give an example.

Large Group Discussion (35 Minutes)

Facilitator: Ask people to gather in one group and discuss the following questions.

1. Tell a story of a Christmas tradition experienced in your past.
2. Name some of the people and some of the events that make God real to you in your life.
3. When you think of the Nativity story, what do you think of—the Christmas tree, being in church, having the family all together, gift giving, etc.?
4. What can be done in our daily lives to develop the sense that Jesus is being born every day to us?
5. Tell a story that makes a connection between caring and nurturing of yourself or someone else, with the scripture passage that says "God-is-with-us."

Wrap-up and Evaluation (5 Minutes)

Facilitator: Has listening to the stories of others helped the group to appreciate the variety of one another's background? Have we been able to focus on the questions and stay on track? Announce that the next session will be a partial "do-it-yourself" session. Over the next couple of years we will learn how to do our own sessions. This first time will be very simple. The theme will be "Christmas Traditions and Self-worth." We'll learn more about it next week. For now just keep the theme in mind. Confirm details for next week. Who will host—bring refreshments—facilitate?

Closing Option (2–4 Minutes)

Facilitator: Reading from next Sunday's scripture.

Refreshments (1/2 hour)

YEAR 2 - F - 6

Theme: Christmas Traditions/Self-worth

Gathering Time—Welcoming and Sharing (10–15 Minutes)

Facilitator: You need to have paper and pencils or pens for everyone. You need to make sure that welcoming and hospitality are going well. Let people become comfortable and talk about their days. Announce the theme and remind people that we are to design some of this session ourselves. After the reading we can break up into three small groups. Each group then will have 25 minutes to think about, discuss and decide on two questions (to be given to another small group) concerning the theme, plus one question for the large group to discuss. The questions should attempt to get people to talk about their traditional experiences of Christmas and how it has affected their self-esteem. Then the groups will exchange questions and dialogue about the questions you receive from the other group. Finally we will come together as a large group to discuss the questions written for them. Who will do our reflection reading after the focus exercise?

Focus Exercise (2–3 Minutes)

A Reading from *A Christmas Carol* by Charles Dickens

(Introduction)

We all know the story of Scrooge in Dickens' *A Christmas Carol*. He was a cold, miserly character who spent his days making money, and his evenings counting all that he made. In a dream he is visited by the spirits of Christmas Past, Christmas Present and Christmas Future, who each reveal how lacking he is in warmth and compassion. Let us join Scrooge toward the end of his dream and interaction with the Ghost of Christmas Future.

"Before I draw nearer to that stone to which you point," said Scrooge, "answer me one question. Are these the shadows of the things that Will be, or are they shadows of things that May be, only."

Still the Ghost pointed to the grave by which it stood.

"Men's courses will foreshadow certain ends, to which, if persevered in, they must lead," said Scrooge. "But if the courses be departed from, the ends will change. Say it is thus with what you show me!"

The Spirit was immovable as ever.

Scrooge crept towards it, trembling as he went; and following the indication of the Spirit, read upon the stone of the neglected grave his own name, EBENEZER SCROOGE...

"Spirit!" he cried, tight clutching at its robe, "hear me! I am not the man I was. I will not be the man I must have been but for this conversation. Why show me this, if I am past hope?"...

Holding up his hands in a last prayer to have his fate reversed, he saw an alteration in the Phantom's hood and dress. It shrunk, collapsed, and dwindled into a bedpost...

Yes! And the bedpost was his own. The bed was his own, the room was his own. Best and happiest of all, the Time before him was his own, to make amends in!
(Pause for a few moments of reflection)

Small Group Discussion (25 Minutes)

Facilitator: Hand out blank sheets of paper and pencils to each of the three small groups. Before breaking into three smaller groups, read the following:

The purpose of this session is to help us share and understand the place Christmas plays in our lives both as a sacred and a secular feast. In developing questions for each group, make sure they are directly related to life experience. Choose questions that are down to earth and not theoretical. Avoid questions that have "yes" or "no" answers.

Some things to consider in making up your questions: Tradition gives meaning to our lives. There are probably more feelings around the traditions of Christmas than any other time of year. We hope to feel good at Christmastime and often experience the opposite. Our self-worth is often undermined by high expectations. Perhaps there are ways of celebrating the holidays that allow for more quality presence and less busyness. Create questions that get at the expectations versus the realities of the holiday.

Think of a question for the large group that is different from the three small group questions, but that sums up or follows from them.

Small Group Discussion (20 Minutes)

Facilitator: Ask the groups to exchange questions and then dialogue about the questions they received.

Large Group Discussion (20 Minutes)

Facilitator: Ask someone from each group to read the large group question. Then facilitate a dialogue about the questions. Rereading a question now and then may help to stay focused.

Wrap-up and Evaluation (5–10 Minutes)

Facilitator: Lead a discussion about the following types of questions. What was it like making up questions? What did you learn in doing it? Did your questions obtain life experiences from people, and help others to reflect on their personal experiences? How did we do in discussing the questions? Announce the theme for the next session, "Is There Life After Christmas?" Confirm details for the next gathering.

Who will host—facilitate—do you want to do something special since this is the end of the quarter? If so plan all the details or make sure everyone is informed.

Closing Options (2–4 Minutes)

Read part of next Sunday's scriptures.

Refreshments (1/2 hour)

YEAR 2 - F - 7

Theme: Is There Life After Christmas?

Gathering Time—Welcoming and Sharing (10 minutes)

Facilitator: Join in the hospitality and welcoming. Make sure everyone is talking and getting comfortable. Announce the theme for the session. You may remind people about the plans (if any) for celebration. Ask someone to read after the focus exercise.

Focus Exercise (2–3 Minutes)

A Reading from *Redemptive Intimacy* by Dick Westley

But how can I tell if I am really walking with the Lord? Easily enough. To walk with the Lord is to have the same effect on people that he did. After encountering us do people feel freer, fear less, walk taller, think nobler, sing more joyfully, and feel more alive than ever before? Do we present an enhancing presence to our world?

(Pause for a few moments of reflection)

Small Group Discussion (20 Minutes)

Facilitator: Ask people to divide into small groups of three and discuss the following questions.

1. How do you feel in looking back on Christmas in previous years in your life?

2. In what ways is Christmas a positive experience for you?

3. In what ways is Christmas a negative experience in your life?

4. Do you enjoy Christmas shopping? Do you set a budget and follow through?

5. Do you give presents with the other person in mind (what they would like) or for yourself, your image?

Large Group Discussion (25 Minutes)

Facilitator: Regather the people and discuss the following questions.

1. Did you identify with other people's stories? If so, in what way?

2. Do you feel you missed some opportunities to make this Christmas season more significant in your life? What can you do to make changes?

3. Reread the Westley reading. Tell about a person you know or have known in the past who had this effect on you.

4. Have you thought that you have this effect on people around you? Can you give an example?

Wrap-up and Evaluation (5–8 Minutes)

Facilitator: Be prepared if the parish wants a written evaluation. We recommend doing this on newsprint so that everyone can be involved and see exactly what is being reported. If there is to be no written report, then a short verbal evaluation of the last set of sessions is important. Remind people that this is our last session, except for whatever celebration may have been planned. However, confirm date, time and place for the first meeting after the new year. Who facilitates, hosts, brings refreshments?

Closing Options (2–4 Minutes)

The scripture reading might be one from the Sunday liturgy, or part of the Christmas readings.

Refreshments (1/2 hour)

Unless a longer celebration has been planned.

YEAR 2 - W - 1

Theme: Reconnections—Refounding

Facilitator: Hospitality is always a key element, especially at new beginnings, from the greeting of people by name at the door, to saying good-bye as each one leaves. Help make sure that everyone is involved in getting and receiving hospitality. Everyone is co-responsible. The facilitator is responsible for coordinating this. The time in parentheses are only guides to keep the group within the 90-minute schedule.

Gathering Time—Welcoming and Sharing (15–20 Minutes)

Facilitator: Make sure everyone is talking and that each person says something about what's been happening in their lives since the last time we met. Announce the theme for the evening. It would be good to briefly review the Guidelines for Sharing, pp. 30–31. Remind everyone of the flow for the evening: A short reflective reading for focusing thoughts, small and large group dialogues, a short wrap-up and a short closing. Ask someone to read after the focus exercise.

Focus Exercise (2–3 Minutes) pp. 31–33

A Reading from *Making Friends with Yourself* by Leo Rock, S.J.

Picture a pond lying there on a windless day. The surface is still. Toss pebbles, one by one, into the center of the pond and each pebble sets in motion a ripple that moves out in ever-widening circles till each gently nudges the edges of the pond…

In spite of all our training, the simple, undeniable fact is that our thoughts on the matter are all that count for us…

Jesus Christ was the greatest pebble-tosser of all time. His pebbles, as all pebbles do, came from the ordinary, the common-place, the familiar—and therefore the timeless. He picked them up wherever he found them: in a wheat field, among a flock of sheep, from children playing in a village square. Jesus knew it was not the pebbles that were important, but those ripples in the mind and heart. We call his word "the living word" precisely because his word has a unique power to set those ripples in motion. The eternal question Jesus puts to us is: Who do you say I am? What do you think? Do you believe? Here, even God's own word defers to what we think.
(Pause for a few moments of reflection)

Small Group Discussion (15–20 Minutes)

Facilitator: Ask the people to break into groups of three and talk about the following questions. Let everyone know you will give them a two-minute signal to allow time to bring their sharing to a conclusion.

1. What has happened to you since the group met? Tell of an episode ("pebble" you tossed). What were the details of the incident, how did you feel, what was its significance?

2. How do you tell your personal story(ies) to other people? Too much, too little detail?

3. Since we last met, how conscious have you been of *values* in your life? What values have you specifically recognized?

Large Group Discussion (20–25 Minutes)

Facilitator: Regather everyone and lead a dialogue about the following questions.

1. How did you receive the story that another person related? Did you listen carefully?

2. How were you able to "read" the other person's feelings? Did you check back with the person to see if you were accurate?

3. What "ripples" does another person's story create for you?

4. Has scripture caused any ripples in your life?

5. Can you learn to read the signs of the "ripples" and figure out what the "pebble" was?

Wrap-up and Evaluation (5 Minutes)

Facilitator: Encourage everyone to talk about this session. How did it go? Were we all sufficiently engaged and engaging? Announce the theme for next week, "Affirmation—Affirming Me, Affirming Us." Confirm the dates, times and details for the next meeting. Who will facilitate, host, bring refreshments?

Closing Options (2–4 Minutes)

Facilitator: Follow your own option. We suggest that a reading from next Sunday's mass be read. Then close with an exchange of the sign of peace.

Refreshments (1/2 hour)

Have refreshments ready in advance. Keep them simple. Help make sure that this stays within the time frame so that people may be on their way.

YEAR 2 - W - 2

Theme: Affirmation—Affirming Me, Affirming Us

Gathering Time—Welcoming and Sharing (10–15 Minutes)

Facilitator: Make sure everyone is welcomed as they arrive. The emphasis is always on hospitality, making people feel comfortable and at ease. Make sure everyone is involved in the conversation about their past week. Announce the theme for the session. Briefly review some part of the Guidelines for Sharing. Ask someone to read after the focus exercise.

Focus Exercise (2–3 Minutes)

A Reading from *Making Friends with Yourself* **by Leo Rock, S.J.**

In real time nothing is ever again. It only seems that way. Today is not a replay of last Thursday, nor is it a preview of next Thursday. The simple truth is that today never happened before nor will it ever happen again. Today is a newly-minted coin that can be spent only once—today; it cannot be hoarded up for future contingencies.

A man took a vacation trip with a friend through the Canadian Rockies. On a wonderfully clear day they rode the aerial tram to the top of a mountain near Jasper. The view was breathtaking: the valley far below with its river winding its way through fields and forest, snow-covered mountains in the surrounding distance. The man said to himself: You will never be here again, so look carefully. He did, and etched indelibly on his memory that magnificent view.

Would we not look more carefully if we remembered that we pass this way only once, that there is no such thing as "again"?
(Pause for a few moments of reflection)

Small Group Discussion (10–25 Minutes)

Facilitator: Ask people to arrange themselves in groups of three for talking about the following questions. Give the groups a two-minute warning before the end of this section to finish their comments.

1. What positive comment has someone made about you in the last year that sticks in your mind? If possible, quote the words. Identify the person who said it along with the situation. What was your reaction?

2. In the last year what is one positive personal comment that you have made to another person? How did the person react? How did that make you feel?

3. When have you not been affirmed, and how did it make you feel?

4. When have you passed up the opportunity to be affirming?

5. Can you name one thing that is etched in your life from last year?

Large Group Discussion (20–25 Minutes)

Facilitator: Regather the large group and facilitate a dialogue on the following questions.

1. Can you think of times when Jesus spoke positive and affirming words to other people? What was the situation and how did the people react to him?

2. What do you need to learn, to develop a habit of making positive comments to others?

3. Go around the group and practice positive comments with one another.

Wrap-up and Evaluation (5 Minutes)

Facilitator: Encourage each person to contribute feedback about the session. Announce the theme for next week, "Reconciliation—The Experience of Limitation."

Confirm the details for the next session. Who will host, facilitate, bring refreshments?

Closing Option (2–4 Minutes)

Refreshments (1/2 hour)

YEAR 2 - W - 3

Theme: Reconciliation—The Experience of Limitation

Gathering Time—Welcoming and Sharing (10–15 Minutes)

Facilitator: Welcoming and hospitality should be easy for everyone to be involved in by this time. The practice here is good preparation for other times for each person. Also the short time to get caught up with each other is important for all. The facilitator is responsible for making sure it all happens. Announce the theme for the session. If there is a point from the Guidelines for Sharing that would be helpful to read or discuss, spend a couple of minutes on that. Who will read after the focus exercise?

Focus Exercise (2–3 Minutes)

A Reading from *Making Friends with Yourself* by Leo Rock, S.J.

While many physical maladies remain, as yet, heartbreakingly incurable, there are many for which we have found the cure. The process involves identifying the malady, isolating the malignant causes, and finding ways to neutralize their destructive action. Sinfulness in all its forms is a spiritual malady—perhaps better said, *the* spiritual malady, ultimately terminal. The temptation is to declare it incurable—at least for the majority of us who cannot afford the expensive and time-consuming cure—and go our merry way. The truth, as revealed by Jesus, is quite otherwise. There is a cure. Faith, hope, and love are cures. Openness to the indwelling Spirit of the Father and the Son is a cure. Openness to the goodness of our inner selves is a cure. The cure is, indeed, expensive, but not beyond our means. The cure does take time, but that's what time is for. Saints are living proof of the curability of the malady. For all of their immense differences from one another, saints have one thing in common: they let God love them and so heal them.
(Pause for a few moments of reflection)

Small Group Discussion (15–20 Minutes)

Facilitator: As usual break into smaller groups of three for talking about the following questions. Let them know you'll give them two minutes of warning before the end of this section. Be aware if groups finish early, or if they need more time.

1. Tell a story of a time when you failed at something.

2. In each story, help each other distinguish why the failure occurred, e.g., was it due to lack of skill, lack of follow-through, commitment or self-sabotage?

3. Do you need to forgive yourself? What helps are there to doing this?

Large Group Discussion (30 Minutes)

Facilitator: Ask everyone to come together again. Read the following about sin and conscience before asking the questions.

1. The action to be a sin must be wrong.

2. The person must know it is wrong.

3. The person chooses to do it and does it.

4. There may be mitigating factors determining the guilt involved.

A definition of conscience from *The Way of Christian Life*:

> The key to any moral decision lies with the individual's conscience, the voice of the reasoning heart. We exercise our conscience by sorting through various moral teachings in order to arrive at a judgment of what we must do concerning the problem at hand. At root, conscience is deciding what "I" must do after making a sincere effort to discover what is right. Our conscience is the primary means by which the Holy Spirit guides us. Because conscience is so allied with the Holy Spirit, it is the most sacred sanctuary within the human person. To violate conscience is to sin.
>
> Conscience is not simply a given of human nature but is formed throughout childhood by genes, nurture and environment. The root of the word "conscience" in Latin means "knowledge together." Formation of conscience is a group activity but in our society we assume it's only a private matter.

Facilitator: Facilitate a dialogue on the following questions.

1. Are there any clarifications needed or any questions about the definition?

2. How do you know when you need to forgive yourself?

3. What role do we, as people of the church, play in society in raising moral issues for society and questions of right and wrong?

4. How do we distinguish between guilt and forgiveness?

Wrap-up and Evaluation (4–5 Minutes)

Facilitator: Encourage each person to contribute feedback in some form about how the session was for them. Did everyone participate well? Did we stay on track? Announce the theme for next week, "Patience and Endurance." Next time is a do-it-yourself session. Does someone want to bring a very brief reading that fits with the theme? Confirm next week—who facilitates, hosts, brings refreshments.

Closing Option (2–4 minutes)

Refreshments (1/2 hour)

YEAR 2 - W - 4

Theme: Patience and Endurance

Gathering Time—Welcoming and Sharing (10–15 Minutes)

Facilitator: For this session you will need to provide paper and pencils. Make sure everyone is welcomed and welcoming. Facilitate the special sharings of the week. Announce the theme and briefly outline the session.

This is a do-it-yourself session. The format will be:

—Work in small groups for 20–25 minutes to write three small group questions and one for the large group.

—Exchange small group questions and discuss them.

—Come back together to discuss large group questions.

This session will focus on our treatment of people we come in contact with, including those close to us and those with whom we have only casual contact, but especially those relationships we find challenging. In developing questions for another group, make sure the questions bring out people's life experiences and don't stay on an abstract level. Avoid questions that can be answered "yes" or "no."

Some definitions to assist us in writing questions are:

ENDURANCE/PATIENCE—the ability to bear difficult and painful situations, relationships; persons with calm stability and perseverance.

RIGHTS/RESPECT—the moral principle of holding the person and property of another as you expect others to respect you and yours.

EQUITY—awareness of the moral and ethical claim of all persons, including one's self, to legal, social and economic equality and fairness, plus a personal commitment to defend this claim. (rf. Hall, Genesis Effect)

Small Group Discussion and Writing (20–25 Minutes)

Facilitator: Ask everyone to break into groups of three. Each group is to discuss and agree on 3 questions for small group dialogue and 1 question to be discussed by the large group. Remember to give the groups a two-minute warning to wrap up this section.

Small Group Discussion (20 Minutes)

Facilitator: Get the groups to exchange questions and dialogue about the questions they receive.

Large Group Discussion (20 Minutes)

Facilitator: Regather the large group and discuss the question written for the large group.

Wrap-up and Evaluation (5–10 Minutes)

Facilitator: How did we do? Ask for specific examples of how people practiced endurance, patience and respect for one another during the session. What is the overall reaction to the session? Announce the theme for next week, "Exodus Journey—Mine and Ours—God's Deliverance." Confirm the details for the next session. Who facilitates, hosts, brings refreshments?

Closing Option (2–4 Minutes)

Facilitator: Your group may be developing its own style by now. We suggest ending with a reading from the scripture from Sunday and a final sign of peace. Whatever you choose, keep it short.

Refreshments (1/2 hour)

YEAR 2 - W - 5

Theme: Exodus Journey—Mine and Ours—God's Deliverance

Gathering Time—Welcoming and Sharing (10–15 Minutes)

Facilitator: Make sure hospitality and welcoming is well done. This should always entail some catching up, sharing daily life and with everyone involved in the dialogue. Announce the theme for the session. Who will read after the focus exercise?

Focus Exercise (2–3 Minutes)

A Reading from Exodus 23:20–22

> See, I am sending an angel before you, to guard you on the way and bring you to the place I have prepared. Be attentive to him and heed his voice. Do not rebel against him, for he will not forgive your sin. My authority resides in him. If you heed his voice and carry out all I tell you, I will be an enemy to your enemies and a foe to your foes.
> (Pause for a short reflection)

Small Group Discussion (20 Minutes)

Facilitator: Ask people to divide into groups of three for talking about the following questions. Let them know you will give a two-minute signal before the end of the discussion.

1. People often learn most from crisis times. Tell of a crisis that you worked through.
2. Who did you talk to about it? Were you honest, did you tell the whole story?
3. Did the other person listen to you? Were they helpful and supportive?

4. At the time did you see God working through other people in helping you to get through this crisis?

Large Group Discussion (20–30 Minutes)

Facilitator: Regather the large group and lead a dialogue about the following questions.

1. What did you learn about yourself as you told your story in the small group?
2. What did you learn about yourself as you listened to the others' stories?
3. Do you get a sense of faith, hope, love from telling of your crisis to another person?
4. How do you see God working in your life in a crisis?

Wrap-up and Evaluation (4–5 Minutes)

Facilitator: Encourage each person to contribute feedback on the session. Did we stay on track or get distracted? Announce the theme for the next session, "I Am Part of a Stiff-necked People—Our Response to God's Deliverance."

Confirm details for the next session. Who will host, facilitate, bring refreshments?

Closing Option (2–4 Minutes)

This should be comfortable for everyone and appropriate to end the session and to prepare for reflections during the coming week.

Refreshments (1/2 hour)

It is important to keep within the time frame so that busy people can keep to their own necessary schedules.

YEAR 2 - W - 6

Theme: I Am Part of a Stiff-necked People —Our Response to God's Deliverance

Gathering Time—Welcoming and Sharing (10–15 Minutes)

Facilitator: Hospitality is basic and everyone is involved by now. This includes a short time of sharing daily happenings. Announce the theme for the session. If there have been any problems within the group you might reread from the Guidelines for Sharing that might apply, with a short discussion. Who will do the reflective reading?

Focus Exercise (2–3 Minutes)

A Reading from Exodus 17:1–3, 23:25–26, 39:42–43

From the desert of Sin the whole Israelite community journeyed by stages, as the LORD directed, and encamped at Rephidim. Here there was no water for the people to drink. They quarreled, therefore, with Moses and said, "Give us water to drink." Moses replied, "Why do you quarrel with me? Why do you put the LORD to a test?" Here, then, in their thirst for water, the people grumbled against Moses, saying, "Why did you ever make us leave Egypt? Was it just to have us die here of thirst with our children and our livestock?"…

…The LORD, your God, you shall worship; then I will bless your food and drink, and I will remove all sickness from your midst; no woman in your land will be barren or miscarry; and I will give you a full span of life…

…The Israelites had carried out all the work just as the LORD had commanded Moses. So when Moses saw that all the work was done just as the LORD had commanded, he blessed them.

(Pause for a short reflection)

Small Group Discussion (15–20 Minutes)

Facilitator: Ask the people to split into two groups and dialogue about the following questions.

1. As Americans, as Catholics, we often think, "We should have it made!" Tell of a time when you were in a situation and wanted to back out. What happened? Did you have a choice, or think you had a choice? Were you encouraged, supported or pushed by others?

2. If you stayed with the situation, did you experience growth from the situation?

Large Group Discussion (30 Minutes)

Facilitator: Regather the group and lead a discussion of the following.

1. What new perspective did you gain as a result of the crisis?
2. In what way did you experience God's deliverance?
3. Is there a situation now that you have difficulty facing? Can you share it?

Wrap-up and Evaluation (5 Minutes)

Facilitator: How did this session go? Were we all encouraging one another, listening to each other? Announce the theme for next week, "Envisioning Jesus."

Next session is the last for this set; how do we want to celebrate?

Confirm all the details for the celebration and the next session. If they are not combined make sure the date and times are clear for everyone.

Who will facilitate and host the celebration if it is separate? Who will facilitate, host and bring refreshments for the next session?

Closing Options (2–4 Minutes)

Refreshments (1/2 hour)

YEAR 2 - W - 7

Theme: Envisioning Jesus

Gathering Time—Welcoming and Sharing (5–10 Minutes)

Facilitator: Make sure that hospitality and welcoming go well. The sharing of daily life is important although this will be shorter this time so that there will be enough time for the rest of the session. Announce the theme. Ask who will read.

Focus Exercise (2–3 Minutes)

A Reading from *Making Friends with Yourself* **by Leo Rock, S.J.**

> The gospel accounts are filled with the encounters that occurred between Jesus and the men and women, even the children, who crossed his path. Encounters with such a different feeling from one to another (in what both Jesus and those he encountered felt), encounters with such varied outcomes. Just like our encounters with those whose paths cross ours. If Jesus was, indeed, as human as we are, his day-by-day interactions with other human beings surely affected how he felt about his day, how he felt about being a human being. Isn't this how it is for us? It is primarily our relationships with one another, not with things, that have the power either to nourish or deplete our spirits. Sunsets and puppy dogs, for all their power to lift our spirits and light our hearts, are not what keep us awake nights with worry or, unless we are born to be hermits, fill our hearts. Only people do that.
>
> (Pause for a short reflection)

Small Group Discussion (20 Minutes)

Facilitator: Ask the people to form groups of three and discuss the following.

1. When you look at another person, do you see Jesus? Give some examples of people you know.
2. Can you think of a time or times in your daily life when Jesus was present in an unexpected way?
3. Give an example from the life of Christ that you can think of, that you would like to emulate/copy? Is there something in your life that Jesus didn't have to face?

Large Group Discussion (30 Minutes)

Facilitator: Ask the people to regather into one group and dialogue about the following questions.

1. How did you relate to other people as they told their stories? Did something they said seem familiar, or similar to what you've experienced or felt?
2. After your small group discussion, *now* who do you say is a good example of Jesus for you?
3. Using your own or another's experience, how do you think Jesus would have faced it? What would he do? What do you do?

Wrap-up and Evaluation (4–5 Minutes)

Facilitator: This may be your celebration, or you may have planned a special time. If so make sure that everything is set for that. Also remind everyone of the date, time and place for the first session of the next set. Who will host, facilitate and bring refreshments? At least who will make sure that these are taken care in the week before it happens.

Closing Option (2–4 Minutes)

Refreshments (1/2 hour)

YEAR 2 - S - 1

Theme: Beginnings—The Age of the Spirit

Gathering Time—Welcoming and Sharing (15–20 Minutes)

Facilitator: As always we focus on hospitality and welcoming, especially at beginnings. Make sure that everyone takes some time to share what has been happening in their lives since we last met, or any important event that they feel is important for them. Be sure everyone talks but keep this section within the time frame. You might mention something that is important from the Guidelines for Sharing which would be helpful. These guidelines should be sort of second nature by this time. They remain important, especially if problems develop. Announce the theme for the evening. Ask someone to do the reading for focusing our thoughts after the focus exercise.

Focus Exercise (2–3 Minutes)

A Reading from Romans 8:13–17

> If you live according to the flesh, you will die; but if by the spirit you put to death the evil deeds of the body, you will live. All who are led by the Spirit of God are sons of God. You did not receive a spirit of slavery leading you back into fear, but a spirit of adoption through which we cry out, "Abba!" (that is, "Father"). The Spirit himself gives witness with our spirit that we are children of God.

> But if we are children, we are heirs as well: heirs of God, heirs with Christ, if only we suffer with him so as to be glorified with him. (Pause for a short reflection time)

Small Group Discussion (30 Minutes)

Facilitator: Ask the people to break into groups of two or three and talk about the following questions.

1. Since we last met, have you gained any new perspectives or had time for reflection about yourself or your life, e.g., your family, school, job, faith? Share whatever you are comfortable with.

2. Did/do you think about your future? Often, seldom? What is the future for you, hope—worry—new beginnings?

3. What does "new beginnings" mean to you—a change of direction in life, more discipline, a new attitude, "resurrection," a change of behavior? Be as specific as you can.

Large Group Discussion and Learning (20 Minutes)

Facilitator: Ask the people to come back into a large group. We suggest that you read the following thoughts, then facilitate a dialogue on the questions.

Learning Reflection

One reason the Jews read scripture was to keep alive the promise of a Messiah. We Christians read the gospels to find Jesus' promise of the Spirit to guide us in bringing the fulfillment of the kingdom. Jesus came as the Christ of history. The church has always taught that the saints are examples of Christ alive in the world for each time and place. Therefore who is "the

Christ" for me today? Who is walking in the footsteps of Jesus here and now?

The Christ is seen amidst all the human giftedness and talent as well as human failings, sins and foibles. So whom do I know who has served as Christ for me? When have I served as Christ for another?

This is a new beginning. Jesus sent the Spirit so the church could come alive. This is the age of the Spirit, when we see and walk with Christ in others, and when we walk as Christ for others.

1. What strikes you about this, or sticks in your mind?
2. In your small group, what thoughts expressed by someone else sounded "familiar" or gave you an insight about yourself?

Wrap-up and Evaluation (5–7 Minutes)

Facilitator: Ask for comments, feedback on the session. These questions are pressing the questions of faith closer to home, to the personal. Personal comments now are important to be heard. Announce the theme for next week, "Awareness of Absence and of Presence." Confirm the details for the next session.

Who hosts, facilitates, brings refreshments?

Closing Options (2–4 Minutes)

Facilitator: By now your group will probably have developed its own ritual. We hope this helps each person enter comfortably into prayer, reflection, as well as focus the group outward toward the larger church and the world.

Refreshments (1/2 hour)

Facilitator: Remember these are to be sim-ple and easily handled so that people can keep the agreed upon time frame.

YEAR 2 - S - 2

Theme: Awareness of Absence and of Presence—The Road to Emmaus

Gathering Time—Welcoming and Sharing (10–15 Minutes)

Facilitator: Continue to facilitate hospitality and welcoming. Encourage a general sharing of the week's happenings. Make sure everyone gets to enter into the conversation. In some way call attention to the Guidelines for Sharing again. Announce the theme. Who will do the reading after the focus exercise?

Focus Exercise (2–3 Minutes)

A Reading from Luke 24:13–35

Two of them that same day were making their way to a village named Emmaus seven miles distant from Jerusalem, discussing as they went all that had happened. In the course of their lively exchange, Jesus approached and began to walk along with them. However, they were restrained from recognizing him. He said to them, "What are you discussing as you go your way?" They halted, in distress, and one of them, Cleopas by name, asked him, "Are you the only resident of Jerusalem who does not know the things that went on there these past few days?" He said to them, "What things?" They said: "All those that had to do with Jesus of Nazareth, a prophet powerful in word and deed in the eyes of God and all the people; how our chief priests and leaders delivered him up to be condemned to death, and crucified him. We were hoping that he was the one who would set Israel free. Besides all this, today, the third day since these things happened, some women of our group have just brought us some astonishing news. They were at the tomb before dawn and failed to find his body, but returned with the tale that they had seen a vision of angels who declared he was alive. Some of our number went to the tomb and found it to be just as the women said, but him they did not see."

Then he said to them, "What little sense you have! How slow you are to believe all that the prophets have announced! Did not the Messiah have to undergo all this so as to enter into his glory?" Beginning, then, with Moses and all the prophets, he interpreted for them every passage of Scripture which referred to him. By now they were near the village to which they were going, and he acted as if he were going farther. But they pressed him: "Stay with us, It is nearly evening—the day is practically over." So he went in to stay with them.

When he had seated himself with them to eat, he took bread, pronounced the blessing, then broke the bread and began to distribute it to them. With that their eyes were opened and they recognized him; whereupon he vanished from their sight. They said to one another, "Were not our hearts burning inside us as he talked to us on the road and explained the Scriptures to us?" They got up immediately and returned to Jerusalem, where they found the Eleven and the rest of the company assembled. They were greeted with, "The Lord has been raised! It is true! He has appeared to Simon." Then they recounted what had happened on the road and how they had come to know him in the breaking of the bread. (Pause for a short reflection)

Large Group Discussion and Learning (20–25 Minutes)

Facilitator: Ask the whole group to dialogue about the following questions.

1. Where is the focus of this story?
2. When does the focus of the story change?

3. What happens when the focus changes in the story?

Facilitator: Read the following paragraphs.

Learning Reflection

The focus of the story is the *past*—two disciples complaining about what has happened. They even connect what happened in the past few days and weeks with scripture—what happened in the distant past. Jesus focuses their attention on the promise, the future, contained in the scripture, the tradition.

The focus of the story makes change possible when the stress becomes more on the *promise* than on the past events. The story really changes when they break bread together, when they nourish each other, when they break bread and share the cup. This event gives them new insights and new inspiration. They are energized and immediately go out to spread the good news.

Small Group Discussion (15–20 Minutes)

Facilitator: Ask the people to break into groups of three and dialogue about the following questions.

1. Where is the focus of *your* life story?
2. Has the focus of your life story ever changed?
3. What happens when the focus of your story changes?

Large Group Discussion and Learning (5–10 Minutes)

Facilitator: Ask the people to reassemble in a large group. Then read the following and facilitate a dialogue and comments about the reflection.

Learning Reflection

This is about the "seeming" absence and the "real" presence. Today many of us focus on God's real presence in the past and the seeming absence in the present. In fact we have the promise that when two or three are gathered in his name, the Spirit makes Christ present, not absent, for us.

Facilitator: Facilitate a dialogue about how we relate to this.

Wrap-up and Evaluation (4–5 Minutes)

Facilitator: Ask people how they feel and what they think about the session. Are the learnings becoming more personal? Announce the session for next week, a do-it-yourself session entitled "Taking a Stand on Faith." This will give some time for preparatory thoughts. Does someone want to bring a brief reading on the theme for next week? Confirm the details for the next session. Who hosts, facilitates, brings refreshments?

Closing Options (2–4 Minutes)

Refreshments (1/2 hour)

YEAR 2 - S - 3

Theme: Taking a Stand on Faith

Gathering Time—Welcoming and Sharing (10–15 Minutes)

Facilitator: You will need to provide paper and pencils for everyone at this session. Make sure that good hospitality and welcoming happens and that everyone is involved in sharing about the past week. Announce the theme and explain that this is a do-it-yourself session. Explain that groups of three will gather to discuss and decide on three questions for another small group as well as one question flowing from them to be discussed by the large group. After exchanging the small group questions they will spend time dialoguing about them. Finally, everyone will gather to discuss the large group questions. Is all this clear? Who will read our beginning reflection?

Focus Exercise (2–3 Minutes)

Learning Reflection

This session will focus on our adult ability to articulate and stand up for our beliefs in a way that does not put others down, but that does not put ourselves down either. In developing questions for another small group, make sure the questions bring out people's life experience. A couple of cautions: Don't ask questions that can be answered "yes" or "no," or questions that are theoretical and don't relate in some way to personal experience.

Here are some definitions that will assist in writing the questions:

PERSONAL AUTHORITY—The freedom to experience and express one's full range of feelings, thoughts and beliefs in a straightforward, objective way, and the confidence that one has a right to be respected for doing so.

EXPRESSIVENESS—To share one's feelings and fantasies so openly and spontaneously that others are free to do the same. (rf. *Genesis Effect*)

Small Group Discussion and Writing (25 Minutes)

Facilitator: Ask people to gather in groups

of three, discuss and decide on three questions. Make sure you have handed out the pencils and paper.

Small Group Discussion (20 Minutes)

Facilitator: Ask the groups to exchange questions and then dialogue about those they receive.

Large Group Discussion (20 Minutes)

Facilitator: Ask everyone to regather into a large group and dialogue about the large group questions.

Wrap-up and Evaluation (5–10 Minutes)

Facilitator: Overall, how did the session go? Ask people if they can give specific instances of how they stood up for what they believe during the session? Was anyone a lone dissenter from the rest of the group? Any other comments?

Announce the theme for next week, "Keeping Alive the Memory—Memory and Presence." Confirm details for the next session. Who will host, facilitate, bring refreshments?

Closing Options (2–4 Minutes)

Facilitator: We hope that a reading from next Sunday's scripture is included in this. The scripture is heard differently after intense spiritual dialogues and in turn hearing the scripture again Sunday makes it richer and deeper. We also hope that a sign of peace is a regular feature.

Refreshments (1/2 hour)

YEAR 2 - S- 4

Theme: Keeping Alive the Memory—Memory and Presence

Gathering Time—Welcoming and Sharing (10–15 Minutes)

Facilitator: Continue to facilitate the practice of hospitality including the sharing of personal daily happenings. Announce the theme for the session. Ask for someone to read.

Focus Exercise (2–3 Minutes)

A Reading from *Through Seasons of the Heart* by John Powell, S.J.

Today's experiences are tomorrow's memories. I think that the most important memory that children carry out of family life is the memory of their parents loving each other. The only people I know who don't believe in love as a permanent thing, as a reliable thing, are people who have never experienced or observed it.

I often go to the gravesides of my grandparents and my parents and I look at those names. I'm named John Powell after my grandfather. I look at "John Powell and Mary Ellen Hardin Powell," and at "Jennie and William Powell." I look at those names and want to say, "Oh, you are not dead. You are not dead because you are surely with God in heaven. I know that. I know you are living, that life was not ended with death but only changed. But I want to tell you something else: you are very much alive in me. All those stories you told me, all those times you shared with me, all the times you held me on your lap—I remember them all. They are alive in me. And I want to thank you. Thank you for so many beautiful memories.
(Pause for a short reflection)

Small Group Discussion (25–30 Minutes)

Facilitator: Ask the people to form groups

of three and discuss the following questions.

1. Think about a story from your past that you could tell—any story that you remember. (Take some time to think about it but don't tell the story.) Talk about the purpose and importance of your memory, of remembering your personal past. What do these memories do to you/for you?

2. Think about something to do with the church in your past (an event, a person, a teaching, but don't tell about it). Talk about the purpose and importance of your remembering, your memories about the church. How do they influence you today?

3. What are some of the memories of yourself that you hope to leave with others and with future generations. Take some time to think about it before answering.

Large Group Discussion and Learning (30–35 Minutes)

Facilitator: Ask the people to regather into one large group then read the following Learning Reflection. After a pause lead a dialogue about the reflection and how it may or may not match personal experiences of the group.

Learning Reflection

Because I remember something, it is significant for me. Remembering reveals something about me to me. It connects me to me, the good and the bad, the liked and the not liked. It connects my present to my past.

   Telling the story connects others to me. Listening to others' stories connects

me to them. Every time we tell the common story of our faith, scripture, tradition, it further connects us to our ancestors and to each other. Telling the story of our ancestors' connection to God in faith further connects me/us to God in faith.

1. What happens when you read scripture? What happens at mass?

2. What memories have been created in you because of your belonging to this parish—with this group?

3. Does your participation in this small group affect your/our participation in mass in any way?

Wrap-up and Evaluation (4–5 Minutes)

Facilitator: Ask the group to reflect back on how the session went. How did we do? Any comments? Announce the theme for the next session, "Common Presence— Communal Living." Confirm the details for the next meeting. Who facilitates, hosts, brings refreshments?

Closing Options (2–4 Minutes)

Refreshments (1/2 hour)

YEAR 2 - S - 5

Theme: Common Presence—Communal Living

Gathering Time—Welcoming and Sharing (10–15 Minutes)

Facilitator: Make sure that your traditions of hospitality and welcoming are carried out. Everyone is co-responsible, you are just the coordinator. Sharing of daily happenings should also be going well with everyone participating. At the appropriate time ask people to get comfortable and announce the theme for the session. Who will read?

Focus Exercise (2–3 Minutes)

A Reading from *Through Seasons of the Heart* by John Powell, S.J.

> An old American Indian saying reminds us that "to truly understand another human being, we must first walk a mile in his moccasins." To this we would like to add the suggestion that we cannot walk in another's moccasins until we first take off our own. We have to make a real effort as listeners to get out of ourselves, to unshackle ourselves from our personal preoccupations, and to donate our presence and availability to others.
>
> At first this will be very difficult, but as with every other human accomplishment, practice will make it easier and easier until it becomes habitual. Presence and availability are very valuable accomplishments, and certainly worth the effort of our repetition and practice.
>
> So let's exchange our shoes and walk a mile together.
> (Pause for a couple of minutes reflection)

Small Group Discussion (6–7 Minutes)

Facilitator: Announce that the small groups will meet twice during this session. At this time they should discuss the first question, then after a large group dialogue, each small group will regather to focus on the second question. For this session a simple way of small group gathering would be to turn to the person next to you and talk about the small group question.

1. In what ways do you live your own life?

Large Group Discussion (6–7 Minutes)

Facilitator: Ask the people to refocus to the large group and continue discussing the same question.

1. In what ways do you live your own life?

Small Group Discussion (6–7 Minutes)

Facilitator: Ask the people to form the same groups, or turn to the same person and discuss the next question.

2. How do you live connected with other people?

Large Group Discussion (40 Minutes)

Facilitator: Ask the people to come back together and dialogue about something that struck each of them from this last small group discussion. After everyone has had a chance to speak continue by reading the following Learning Reflection.

Learning Reflection

We have to tell our stories to be present—to ourselves and to others. I have to listen to others' stories to be present to them as they are present to themselves. Stories help me and others see the whole of me—where I come from and where I'm going. The present is the overlap between the two large "plates" (e.g., tectonic) called "past" and "future."

3. What are the consequences of not telling our stories, of not being really present to self or to others? Give an example.
4. What are the consequences of not listening as others tell their stories? Give an example.

Wrap-up and Evaluation (4–5 Minutes)

Facilitator: Ask people to give their reaction to the session. How did the different format work? Ask for other comments. Announce the theme for next session, "Ordinary and Extraordinary Presence—All the Saints." Confirm the details for next time. Who facilitates, hosts, brings refreshments?

Closing Options (2–4 Minutes)

Refreshments (1/2 hour)

YEAR 2 - S - 6

Theme: Ordinary and Extraordinary Presence—All the Saints

Gathering Time—Welcoming and Sharing (10–15 Minutes)

Facilitator: As usual make sure that the gathering time is coordinated for hospitality and welcoming. Announce the theme for the week.

Focus Exercise (2–3 Minutes)

Small Group Discussion (30 Minutes)

Facilitator: Ask the people to form small groups of two or three and dialogue about the following questions.

1. Who and/or what has provided the greatest sense of belonging for you?
2. What were the actions that permitted/encouraged that happening?
3. In what sense are they ordinary things, events, actions? In what sense are they extraordinary?

Large Group Discussion and Learning (35 Minutes)

Facilitator: Ask the people to regather into one group then read the following reflec-

tion. (Or you may ask if someone else wants to read.) After a slight pause facilitate a dialogue about the following questions.

Learning Reflection

Jesus was known as an ordinary man. The first thirty years are obscure (ordinary). The first two chapters of two gospels are a small exception. These are to make theological points.

Other questions also reveal Jesus' ordinariness, "Who is the Nazarene?" "Isn't this the carpenter's son?" Yet the ordinary life of Jesus more and more revealed the extraordinary life of God.

Jesus chose ordinary disciples: fishermen, a tax collector, zealots, a reformed sinner (prostitute), mothers, etc. They in turn became extraordinary people.

1. Where do we usually look for the extraordinary? Can you give an example?
2. How can you learn to get past ordinary time to extraordinary time?
3. How can you see beyond the ordinary person to the extraordinary presence in your life?

Wrap-up and Evaluation (10 Minutes)

Facilitator: Ask about the reaction to the session. What new thoughts does anyone have? Are there new insights? Announce the theme for next week, "Together for the Long Haul—Ordinary Time." Since that is the last session for this year do we want a special celebration. You might want to have a longer session or have a special celebration session. This may have become customary by now for your group. Confirm all the details for the celebration and the last session. Who hosts next, facilitates, brings desert?

Also the parish may want a special evaluation (sometimes written). If so be prepared to write some of it down, or fill out their form at the end session. It is always good for the group and for the parish to keep a written reminder of what has gone on.

Closing Options (2–4 Minutes)

Refreshments (1/2 hour)

YEAR 2 - S - 7

Theme: Together for the Long Haul—Ordinary Time

Gathering Time—Welcoming and Sharing (10–15 Minutes)

Facilitator: Since this is the last session all should go well about hospitality, since everyone is practiced and participating by now. Announce the theme for the session.

Focus Exercise (2–3 Minutes)

Small Group Discussion (10–15 Minutes)

Facilitator: Ask the people to divide into groups of three and discuss the following questions.

1. How has "having your act together" helped you in relating—being together with others?
2. How has your not "having your act together" hindered your being together with others?

3. Who has helped you get your act together? Describe.

Large Group Discussion and Learning (40 Minutes)

Facilitator: Ask the people to regather into a large group and ask someone to read the following. Then lead a dialogue on the following questions.

Learning Reflection

Getting my life totally together is impossible now. Living with others who are totally together is a flight of fantasy. Balance is the integration of all the aspects of our lives. It is difficult to keep balance.

1. What does it mean to "lurch from the pits to the peaks" or crisis to crisis, rather than to keep your balance in life? Can you tell about a time when you did this?
2. Can you think of one thing in your life you can change, or ways you could act differently with others—from this session—from this quarter—from this group?
3. Until we meet again, for you, what do you want to say to this group?

Wrap-up and Evaluation (5–7 Minutes)

Facilitator: It is helpful for the group and the parish to record year-end evaluations. Confirm the celebration details. Plan for means of contact for next fall's set of sessions.

Closing Options (4–5 Minutes)

Refreshments (1/2 hour)

CHAPTER 6

YEAR 3 - F - 1

Theme: Reconnections/Refounding—Catching Up with Each Other

Gathering Time—Welcoming and Introductions (15–20 Minutes)

Facilitator: Group members by this time will have realized they are all co-responsible for hospitality and greeting, you are the coordinator of it. After chatting about their day, announce the theme for the session. Remind the group of the Guidelines for Sharing, pp. 30-31, and read any parts that you think might be helpful. You should have newsprint, masking tape, and a marker ready to be used in the large group discussion.

Focus Exercise (2–3 Minutes), pp. 31–33.

Small Group Discussion (20–25 Minutes)

Facilitator: Ask the people to break into small groups and talk about the following question.

1. Tell about three events that were significant for you since we last met. What made them significant for you?

Large Group Discussion (40 Minutes)

Facilitator: Ask the people to come together into one group to discuss the following questions. You probably will want someone to record the ideas from question three.

1. Describe one significant event related by another member in your group.
2. What do you think it meant to the other person telling the story and what did it mean to you?
3. What did it mean to you when another person told your story? How did you feel?
4. After being together for two years, and reflecting back on your experiences, what do you expect to happen this set of sessions, or in the future?

Wrap-up and Evaluation (5–10 Minutes)

Facilitator: Spend some time in reviewing the session. Did you have difficulty picking up again in the groups? Make sure everyone has a chance to make comments. Announce the theme for next time, "Acceptance of What Is, Who Is and What Has Been." Confirm all the details, date, time, place, especially who hosts, brings refreshments and facilitates.

Closing Options (2–4 Minutes)

The group may want to continue past practices. It is good to shift occasionally. We recommend scripture reading from the next Sunday liturgy.

Refreshments (1/2 hour)

Enjoy, socialize and finish on time.

YEAR 3 - F - 2

Theme: Acceptance of What Is, Who Is and What Has Been

Gathering Time—Welcoming and Sharing (15–20 Minutes)

Facilitator: This is the co-responsibility of everyone. Make sure that people are beginning to focus by talking about their personal experiences of the day. After people have checked in announce the theme for the session.

Focus Exercise (2–3 Minutes)

Small Group Discussion (20 Minutes)

Facilitator: Ask the people to break into small groups (2–3 persons) and dialogue about the following questions.

1. Tell about a time when you felt connected to other people. Tell about a time when you felt disconnected with others. How did you feel and how did you act?

2. Describe a time when you were with someone or in a group and really wished you were somewhere else. How did you act? Did you or could you have done something to interact better or more fully?

Large Group Discussion (40–60 Minutes)

Facilitator: Ask the people to gather as one large group. Read the following slowly, pausing briefly afterward. Then facilitate a dialogue about the following questions.

Learning Reflection

Real listening and accepting are not attained easily. We need discipline and practice to be present, to accept what is and what has been.

1. What do you notice about the body language of others in this group, now and from previous sessions? What is your body language? Is it reflecting what you are feeling or thinking?

2. When someone speaks, how do they know you're listening?

3. If distracting thoughts enter your mind how do you let them be and let them go?

4. Was there a time when you were really distracted in a situation or with someone? What did you do?

Wrap-up and Evaluation (7–10 Minutes)

Facilitator: Spend some time critiquing the session. Does anyone have anything they would like to say or question that has not been said? Announce that next week will be a do-it-yourself session and the theme will be "Social Prestige." Confirm all the details, date, place, time, who hosts, facilitates and brings refreshments.

Closing Options (2–4 Minutes)

These are important but should be very short and comfortable for everyone.

Refreshments (1/2 hour)

Enjoy!

YEAR 3 - F - 3

Theme: Social Prestige

Gathering Time—Welcoming and Sharing (15–20 Minutes)

Facilitator: You will need to provide paper and pencils for this session. But make sure the hospitality and greeting go well.

Announce the theme for the session and that this is a do-it-yourself session. The outline will be:

—work in small groups to develop a set of four questions for other groups, plus one question for the large group.

—exchange questions and discuss them in small groups.

—discuss questions in the large group, then evaluate how it worked.

Ask someone to do the reading after the focus exercise.

Focus Exercise (2–3 Minutes)

Facilitator: Read the following slowly as the process begins.

Learning Reflection

Think of the ways we have been socialized to live in this society, from the way we speak, the way we dress, to the way we act and carry ourselves. Some of this has come through parental influence, some through our teachers, some through peer pressure. The people who are important to us exert an ongoing influence through their expectations. When we meet these expectations we gain social prestige.

(Pause)

In writing questions, think of ones that will stimulate discussion on the uses and abuses of social prestige in society, church, family, peer groups and among friends. Pull these out of your own experiences. Word the questions to ensure they invite personal life experiences in response. Be careful not to use leading questions. An example of a leading question would be, "Don't you think it's wrong to use social prestige to make a lot of money?"

Definitions of social prestige are "personal appearance which reflects success and achievement and gains the esteem of others; respect and validation coming from one's peers which is necessary for one to grow and succeed."

Small Group Writing (20 Minutes)

Facilitator: Hand out paper and pencils as you ask people to divide into groups of three, and write four small group questions and one for the large group.

Small Group Discussion (15–20 Minutes)

Facilitator: Ask the groups to exchange questions to be discussed. Give a couple of minutes warning for finishing the discussion.

Large Group Discussion (15–20 Minutes)

Facilitator: Ask people to gather into a large group and facilitate a dialogue about the questions that each group has developed. You may not be able to do all the questions. It is important to keep the dialogue coming from personal experiences.

Wrap-up and Evaluation (7–10 Minutes)

Facilitator: Ask how did it go. Did the questions bring out the responses you expected? Did the questions get people talking about their own experiences?

Announce the theme for the next session, "Faith and Risk—New Challenges." Confirm the details for the next session: date, time, place, who facilitates, brings refreshments and hosts.

Closing Options (2–4 Minutes)

Refreshments (1/2 hour)

YEAR 3 - F - 4

Theme: Faith and Risk—New Challenges

Gathering Time—Welcoming and Sharing (10–15 Minutes)

Facilitator: Make sure greeting and hospitality go well. After appropriate mingling and chatting about the day announce the theme for the session. You can do the reading or ask someone else to do it after the focus exercise.

Focus Exercise (2–3 Minutes)

Learning Reflection

Risk is the active verb of creating the future. Risk means accepting the consequences of one's decisions and actions. The ability to risk depends on faith in the present and hope in a positive future. (Suffering can be part of a positive future.)

Worry is refusing to accept responsibility/accountability for the future. Worry is the refusal to accept the consequences of my decisions and actions.

Faith is always in the present. Faith is accepting the present as good. Faith is accepting the present with all of its gifts and limitations.

Small Group Discussion (15–20 Minutes)

Facilitator: Ask people to divide into groups of three and talk about the following questions.

1. When have you experienced faith in your life?
2. Tell of a time when you complained about the present.
3. Tell of a time when you worried about the future.

4. Tell a story relating a time when you took a risk and why?

Large Group Discussion (40 Minutes)

Facilitator: Ask people to return to one group and dialogue about the following questions.

1. What do you spend most of your time on, faith and hope or worry and complaining? Can you think of an example?
2. Do faith/hope or worry/complaining energize or challenge you? Give examples.
3. What did Jesus come to teach us?
4. Tell a story about someone you know who took a risk and the consequences, e.g., a family member, friend, parishioner.

Wrap–up and Evaluation (5–7 Minutes)

Facilitator: Ask everyone to comment about the session. What were some of the things learned? Announce the theme for the next session, "Communal Prayer, Now and Forever." Confirm the details for the next meeting, especially hosting, facilitating and bringing refreshments.

Closing Options (2–4 Minutes)

Refreshments (1/2 hour)

YEAR 3 - F - 5

Theme: Communal Prayer, Now and Forever—All the Saints

Gathering Time—Welcoming and Sharing (10–15 Minutes)

Facilitator: After appropriate hospitality

and welcoming time announce the theme for the session. Ask someone to read the selection below.

Focus Exercise (2–3 Minutes)

Learning Reflection

Communal prayer involves more than one person; it is more powerful than the sum of the individual parts. Communal prayer depends on common sound, common sight and common action. The presence of others helps a person to be more present. Communal prayer brings a connectedness to others and to God. This type of prayer is always a sensory experience. It pulls us into the present while recalling the past and anticipating the future. Therefore this prayer connects all times and all people. Communal prayer is the connection of the faithful with the Communion of Saints.

Small Group Discussion (15 Minutes)

Facilitator: Ask people to break into groups of three and discuss the following questions.

1. What images, symbols, experiences come to mind when you hear the words "communal prayer"?

2. Take one of these images and describe more fully; include sights, sounds, smells, taste.

Large Group Discussion (40 Minutes)

Facilitator: Ask the people to come together for a dialogue about the following questions.

1. Do you expect any sensory experiences in communal prayer? For example?

2. Are there some sensory experiences in communal prayer that you find

uncomfortable, distracting, etc.? Explain.

3. Reflecting upon the experiences we have just shared, what can we do to make our group prayer more balanced and spiritually nourishing for one another?

4. Is there something we can do to make the parish communal prayer experiences, particularly the mass, richer and more meaningful for us and for the whole community?

Wrap-up and Evaluation (5–7 Minutes)

Facilitator: Invite feedback about the session. Are there more things that need to be said before we leave? Announce the theme for the next session, "Thanksgiving/Getting." Ask someone in the group to bring a written brief history of Thanksgiving next week and be prepared to read it to the group. Confirm all the details for the next time. Who will host, bring refreshments, facilitate?

Closing Options (2–4 Minutes)

Refreshments (1/2 hour)

YEAR 3 - F - 6

Theme: Thanksgiving/Getting

Gathering Time—Welcoming and Sharing (10–15 Minutes)

Facilitator: You will need to provide paper and pencils for this session. Attend to shepherding the hospitality and talking about the day's cares. Announce the theme of the session.

Focus Exercise (2–3 Minutes)

Small Group Discussion (20 Minutes)

Facilitator: Ask the people to divide into small groups and talk about the following questions.

1. Talk about a time when you gave thanks for what you were given. Talk about a time when you gave thanks for what you didn't get.

2. Tell about a time when you didn't get something you prayed for and were thankful about afterwards.

3. Is there anything that's happened in your life that you didn't ask for, or expect, yet now you're thankful it happened?

Large Group—Personal Journal (5 Minutes)

Facilitator: Ask the people to gather in one group, give out paper and pencils and ask them to privately reflect on "How do I give thanks"?

A History of Thanksgiving and Discussion (30 Minutes)

Facilitator: Ask the person who prepared the Thanksgiving history to read it to the group. Then facilitate a dialogue with the following questions.

1. What were some of the significant things said in your small group and how can you relate to them?

2. Did anything in the Thanksgiving story that was read strike you as significant?

3. How do we individually and in groups, e.g., family, parish, etc., give thanks today?

Wrap-up and Evaluation (5–7 Minutes)

Facilitator: Let people critique the session. How did it go? Are we learning how to keep the meetings going and share our learning experiences? Announce the theme for next session, "Perception, Patience and Waiting." That will be the last session for this set, so should we have a special celebration? Confirm the date and way of celebrating as well as for the next session.

Closing Options (2–4 Minutes)

Facilitator: Since the theme for today is special we suggest a corresponding special prayer format. Use the following reading, or any of the selections from pp. 142–149 or any other you think best for your group.

A Reading from Philippians 4:4-7

> Rejoice in the Lord always! I say it again: Rejoice! Everyone should see how unselfish you are. The Lord is near. Dismiss all anxiety from your minds. Present your needs to God in every form of prayer and in petitions full of gratitude. Then God's own peace, which is beyond all understanding, will stand guard over your hearts and minds, in Christ Jesus.

Let each person offer personal prayers of Thanksgiving.

End with a Sign of Peace.

Refreshments (1/2 hour)

YEAR 3 - F - 7

Theme: Perception, Patience and Waiting

Gathering Time—Welcoming and Sharing (15–20 Minutes)

Facilitator: After the hospitality and daily

sharing announce the theme for the session. Ask someone to do the reading later on.

Focus Exercise (2–3 Minutes)

Small Group Discussion (20 Minutes)

Facilitator: Ask the people to divide into small groups and talk about the following questions.

1. Tell of a time when you were patient with yourself or another person. What were the circumstances?
2. Can you give an example of when you were impatient with another person or persons? With yourself?
3. Do you think God is ever impatient with you? Talk more about this.

A Reading from Mark 1:2–5, 7–8

> In Isaiah the prophet it is written: "I send my messenger before you to prepare your way: a herald's voice in the desert, crying, 'Make ready the way of the Lord, clear him a straight path.'" Thus it was that John the Baptizer appeared in the desert, proclaiming a baptism of repentance which led to the forgiveness of sins. All the Judean countryside and the people of Jerusalem went out to him in great numbers....
>
> The theme of his preaching was: "One more powerful than I is to come after me. I am not fit to stoop and untie his sandal straps. I have baptized you in water; he will baptize you in the Holy Spirit."
> (Pause for a few moments)

Large Group Discussion (40 Minutes)

Facilitator: Lead a discussion of the following questions.

1. What are the signs that God is present (incarnated/enfleshed) in the world today?
2. Tell about a time of waiting for some-

thing, someone. What function does this experience of waiting serve in your life?

3. Tell about a time you abstained from something. What function does abstinence serve in your life?
4. Do you think "abstinence makes the heart grow fonder"? Is there something you can do to keep this group close to your mind and heart in the coming weeks?

Wrap-up and Evaluation (5–7 Minutes)

Facilitator: Let the group think back through the various parts of the session. Was everyone involved, heard and listened to? Are there any comments about this set of sessions you'd like to make? The parish may want a report, so be prepared to give that if asked. Carry out whatever celebrations you had planned.

Closing Options (2–4 Minutes)

Refreshments (1/2 hour)

YEAR 3 - W - 1

Theme: Reconnecting Our Giftedness

Gathering Time—Welcoming and Sharing (15–20 Minutes)

Facilitator: We will always focus on hospitality and welcoming by making sure that everyone is greeted and spends some time talking about what has been happening to them recently. Be sure everyone talks about their week but stays within the time frame and starts on time. Since this is the beginning of a new set of meetings you might want to read the Guidelines for Sharing, pp. 30–31 (or at least some important part). Announce the theme for the evening. Ask someone to do the reading for the focusing of our thoughts after the focus exercise.

Focus Exercise (2–3 Minutes)

A Reading from Matthew 2:1–2, 7–11

> After Jesus' birth in Bethlehem of Judea during the reign of King Herod, astrologers from the east arrived one day in Jerusalem inquiring, "Where is the newborn King of the Jews? We observed his star at its rising and have come to pay him homage."…
>
> Herod called the astrologers aside and found out from them the exact time of the star's appearance. Then he sent them to Bethlehem, after having instructed them: "Go and get detailed information about the child. When you have found him, report it to me so that I may go and offer him homage too."
>
> After their audience with the king, they set out. The star which they had observed at its rising went ahead of them until it came to a standstill over the place where the chld was. (Pause for a short reflective time)

Large Group Discussion (30 Minutes)

Facilitator: Have the whole group dialogue about the following questions.

1. Other than material gifts, what human gifts did you receive at Christmas and during the holidays?
2. What gift of yourself did you *give?* Tell the story, the situation, who the person or people in the situation were.

Small Group Discussion (10 Minutes)

Facilitator: Ask the people to break into groups of two or three and talk about the following question.

1. What happened that was significant for you since we last met?

Large Group Discussion (30 Minutes)

Facilitator: Ask the people to gather again as one group and discuss the following questions.

1. Over the holidays, what made you comfortable, feel good?
2. Over the holidays what got you excited?
3. Did you make any New Year's resolutions? What practical steps do you have to carry them out? What can we do to help one another to keep the resolutions?

Wrap-up and Evaluation: (3–5 Minutes)

Facilitator: Spend some time in reviewing how the session went. Try to get everyone to enter into the discussion. Announce the theme for next week, "Our Giftedness for Others—Service, Ecumenism, Evangelization." Check who will host the next session, who will facilitate and who will bring refreshments.

Closing Options (2–4 Minutes)

Facilitator: You may have developed your preferences by now. We recommend that you use one of the readings from Sunday's scriptures with a minute or two of quiet afterward.

Refreshments (1/2 hour)

Facilitator: Make sure that these stay simple and easily handled so that people can socialize and still keep to the time frame and leave.

YEAR 3 - W - 2

Theme: Our Giftedness for Others—Service, Ecumenism, Evangelization

Gathering Time—Welcoming and Sharing (20 Minutes)

Facilitator: As everyone enters it should be routine that they are welcomed and sharing about their week. Announce the theme for the evening and ask everyone to assemble. If there is any need, read part of the Guidelines for Sharing. Tell everyone that this evening we will not have a reflective reading, but will begin with a dialogue.

Focus Exercise (2–3 Minutes)

Large Group Discussion (15–20 Minutes)

Facilitator: Lead a dialogue about the following questions.

1. Turn to the person next to you and talk about "What are my gifts for others?"

2. As a group, talk about the gifts you see in the person with whom you just shared.

Reading and Reflection (7–8 Minutes)

Facilitator: Ask someone to read the following quotations. After a time of silence ask people to speak out their reflections initiated by the readings.

A Reading from the *Documents of Vatican II*, "Decree on the Apostolate of the Laity"

> For the exercise of this apostolate, the Holy Spirit who sanctifies the People of God through the ministry and the sacraments gives to the faithful special gifts as well, (cf. 1 Cor. 12:7), "allotting to everyone according as he will" (1 Cor. 12:11). Thus may the individual, "according to the gift that each has received, administer it to one another" and become "good stewards of the manifold

> grace of God" (1 Pet. 4:10), and build up thereby the whole body in charity (cf. Eph. 4:16). From the reception of these charisms or gifts, including those which are less dramatic, there arise for each believer the right and duty to use them in the church and in the world for the good of mankind and for the upbuilding of the Church. In so doing, believers need to enjoy the freedom of the Holy Spirit who "breathes where he wills" (Jn. 3:8). (Pause briefly)

"Decree on Ecumenism"

> The "ecumenical movement" means those activities and enterprises which, according to various needs of the church and opportune occasions, are started and organized for the fostering of unity among Christians. These are: first, every effort to eliminate words, judgments, and actions which do not respond to the condition of separated brethren with truth and fairness and so make mutual relations between them more difficult; then, "dialogue" between competent experts from different Churches and Communities....Through such dialogue, everyone gains a truer knowledge and more just appreciation of the teaching and religious life of both Communions. In addition, these Communions cooperate more closely in whatever projects a Christian conscience demands for the common good. (Pause briefly)

Small Group Discussion (35–40 Minutes)

Facilitator: After most people have spoken personal words of reflection ask the people to break into groups of two or three for further dialogue. Then ask the reader to reread the two readings without the pauses. Read the following statements and then discuss the questions below.

Evangelization—(is) Telling my story of the good news.

Ecumenism—(is) Reaching out and cooperating with other Christian churches.

Reconciliation—(is) Seeking out those who are apart for whatever reason and creating a space for peace and healing, for them and for ourselves.

1. What is the connection between the gifts we talked about last week and baptismal gifts?
2. How do evangelization, ecumenism, and reconciliation relate to personal gifts and baptismal gifts?
3. Talk about a time when you used your personal gifts in service for others.
4. Tell a story about a time when you were involved in either an ecumenical or evangelizing situation. What gifts did you use?

Wrap-up and Evaluation (5–7 Minutes)

Facilitator: Ask for comments on the session. This has been a complex evening and there are a great variety of points and learning that people may have gotten. Be careful that people do not feel overwhelmed but that something clicked for each. Announce the theme for the next session, "Physical Delight—Confidence and Competence." Confirm the details for next week. Who hosts, brings refreshments and facilitates?

Closing Options (2–4 Minutes)

Facilitator: We suggest readings from the next Sunday's mass, or prayer suggestions on pp. 27–30, if you do not have a routine of closing prayers for your group.

Refreshments: (1/2 hour)

Facilitator: Make sure that everyone is socializing well and that they are able to leave within the time frame.

YEAR 3 - W - 3

Theme: Physical Delight—Confidence and Competence

Gathering Time—Welcoming and Sharing (20 Minutes)

Facilitator: For this session you will need to supply paper and pencils. Make sure everyone is welcomed. Gather the people and if there is a need go over some part of the Guidelines for Sharing. Announce that this will be a do-it-yourself session. Briefly outline the time as follows.

—Meet in small groups for 20–25 minutes to create three small group questions.
—Exchange small group questions and discuss for 20 minutes.
—Discuss large group questions.

Reflection Time (3–4 Minutes)

Facilitator: Ask someone to read the following.

This session will focus on our existence in this world as enfleshed spirits, as body-persons with abilities to delight in the world around us through our senses and to accomplish things in the world through work.

Some definitions to assist in drawing up questions are:

SENSORY PLEASURE: Physical delight through the senses—sight, sound, smell, taste, touch.

COMPETENCE/CONFIDENCE: Realistic and objective confidence that one has the skills to achieve in the world of work and to feel that the achievement is a positive contribution. (rf. *Genesis Effect*)

Small Group Writing (20 Minutes)

Facilitator: Make sure that everyone has paper and pencil. Ask the people to divide into groups of two or three and from their dialogue on the topic and definitions write three questions for another small group to discuss. We will not need questions for a large group this evening.

Small Group Discussion (20 Minutes)

Facilitator: Ask the groups to exchange questions and discuss the ones they receive.

Large Group Discussion (20 Minutes)

Facilitator: Gather the people back for a large group discussion. Ask the group to talk about some specific instances of their sense recognition this evening (e.g., comfortable chair, difficultly in hearing, etc.). A discussion of the place, time, development and use of the senses may help fill out this session. Keep it always to personal specifics will keep the group focused.

Wrap-up and Evaluation (5–7 Minutes)

Facilitator: Get the group to talk about how it worked tonight, writing the questions and others' responses to the questions as they were discussed, etc. This is a new phase of our learning. What can we look forward to improving our next do-it-yourself session?

Announce the theme for next week, "Cleaning House—Sorting Our Baggage." Confirm the details for next time: date, place for hosting as well as who facilitates, brings refreshments.

Closing Options (2–4 Minutes)

Facilitator: There are several options to choose from. We highly recommend a reading of one of the coming Sunday liturgy readings.

Refreshments (1/2 hour)

Facilitator: This is a very important time to wind down, mingle and get ready to depart, so that people can get on with the rest of their busy lives.

YEAR 3 - W - 4

Theme: Cleaning House—Sorting Our Baggage

Gathering Time—Welcoming and Sharing (15–20 Minutes)

Facilitator: (Note: This session is suited for pre-Lent or the beginning of Lent. You may want to adjust your schedule accordingly.)

Make sure that the hosting and welcoming is going well. Announce the theme of the session. If you think it appropriate, go over some part of the Guidelines for Sharing. Ask someone to do the reading.

Focus Exercise (2–3 Minutes)

Large Group Discussion (10 Minutes)

Facilitator: Get the whole group involved in talking about the following question.

1. When is your spiritual housecleaning "out with the cobwebs"? How and when do you do it?

Small Group Discussion (30 Minutes)

Facilitator: Ask the people to break into groups of two or three and suggest they take 15 minutes for questions 1 and 2 below and then another 15 minutes for questions 3 and 4. You should give them a mid-point reminder to switch.

1. Talk about a time of housecleaning—when you were making decisions on what items to throw out, what to keep.
2. How did you do the sorting? What priorities did you use in deciding what to keep and what to throw away?
3. Tell of a time when you did this process of sorting, keeping and throwing out with your life.
4. What criteria did you use to help in sorting out your life?

Large Group Discussion (20 Minutes)

Facilitator: Gather the whole group for a discussion of the following questions.

1. What criterion do you use to sort out your spiritual life? Where did this criterion come from? How did you decide if it was good or bad?
2. What is the resistance you have to cleaning and sorting in your spiritual life?
3. What are some helps in implementing our spiritual housecleaning?
4. What are ways we can help one another in this sorting?

Wrap-up and Evaluation (5–7 Minutes)

Facilitator: Take time to ask people how they would evaluate the session. Were the questions helpful? After a short discussion announce the theme for the next session, "Worship—Me/We." Confirm the date and host for the next meeting as well as who will facilitate and who will bring refreshments.

Closing Options (2–4 Minutes)

Facilitator: Ask someone to read one of the next Sunday mass readings or whatever is comfortable for the group.

Refreshments (1/2 hour)

YEAR 3 - W - 5

Theme: Worship—Me/We

Gathering Time—Welcoming and Sharing (15–20 Minutes)

Facilitator: As always, welcoming and hospitality are very important at the beginning of every meeting. After people have talked about their day, their immediate concerns and become seated, announce the theme for the session. Ask someone to read the following reflection.

Focus Exercise (2–3 Minutes)

Learning Reflection

As members of the mystical body of Christ, no one of us is ever alone at mass. We are not only in communion with those physically present but also with all those who have gone before and all who are yet to be. Even when mass is over each one carries the community of saints with us in our hearts and minds. This mystical communion of saints is never complete without each of us. (Pause for two to three minutes)

Small Group Discussion (25–30 Minutes)

Facilitator: Ask the group to divide into groups of two or three and dialogue about the following questions.

1. Do you have a certain pattern in your prayer life? For example, a special place, the same time of day, specific prayers that you recite, etc.
2. Do you have a certain pattern in your public prayer, such as sitting in the same

pew, with the same people, attending the same mass, arriving early—or late, staying to chat or rushing out the door?

3. What kind of connections do you see between your public and private prayer?

4. Describe any powerful group ritual that you have experienced. What were the elements, what was done (actions, sights, sounds, words) that made it powerful?

Large Group Discussion (30 Minutes)

Facilitator: Gather the people back into one large group and discuss the following questions.

1. How are you most affirmed as a person when participating in group ritual?

2. How are you touched by others in group ritual? What connections are there between these two questions?

3. How does my participation or lack of participation affect others within group ritual (the "me" in the "we")?

4. How does the participation of others or lack of it, affect me within group ritual (the "we" in the "me")?

5. In what ways have you felt changed by the rituals you talked about?

Wrap-up and Evaluation (5–7 Minutes)

Facilitator: Ask the group to think back through the session. How did things go? Was everyone involved, listened to? Announce the theme for the next session, "Worship—Law/Spirit or You Can't Keep Good Worship Quiet." Confirm the details for the next time: date, place, host, facilitator, refreshments.

Closing Options (2–4 Minutes)

Facilitator: It is good to keep the same rituals, because this makes people comfortable. However, there may come a time when a switch for some reason or some time may be appropriate. Occasionally check this out with the people in the group.

Refreshments (1/2 hour)

YEAR 3 - W - 6

Theme: Worship—Law/Spirit or You Can't Keep Good Worship Quiet

Gathering Time—Welcoming and Sharing (15–20 Minutes)

Facilitator: The welcoming and hospitality will take care of itself by now but you should be alert to any needs. Announce the theme for the session.

Focus Exercise (2–3 Minutes)

Facilitator: Ask someone to read the following and follow it by 2–3 minutes of silence.

Learning Reflection

The community of saints is present when we are gathered together in community worship. Liturgy formally begins when we gather at church and formally ends with the end of the liturgy. However, it continues through the farewells after mass, conversing over coffee and donuts, in the parking lot, and on into the week.

Large Group Discussion (10 Minutes)

Facilitator: Ask the following question of

the entire group and facilitate a dialogue about it.

1. Can we bring together the themes of the last two sessions?

The themes were "Cleaning House, Sorting Our Baggage" and "Worship—Me/We." What do you recall about our discussions, what were some of the key points?

Small Group Discussion (7–8 Minutes)

Facilitator: Ask people to turn to one other person and discuss the following questions.

1. What personal preparation do you make for mass, both before and after your arrival at the church?

2. For you what are the essential parts of the mass?

Small Group Discussion (20–25 Minutes)

Facilitator: Ask each group of two to join with another group of two and discuss the following questions.

3. How does the Holy Spirit speak through community worship to you? How does the Holy Spirit speak through you to the community?

4. How does the Holy Spirit speak through this group to you?

5. How does the Holy Spirit speak to this group through you?

Large Group Discussion (25 Minutes)

Facilitator: Ask the people to reassemble into a large group and dialogue about the following questions.

1. How do the various parts of your week relate to participation at Sunday mass—for example, your participation in this group?

2. What makes the difference between going though the motions at Sunday mass and having a meaningful experience?

3. What can you do to become more conscious of the community aspect of prayer, ritual, mass?

4. How can we as church maintain the balance between the individual person and the assembly for our worship?

Wrap-up and Evaluation (5–6 Minutes)

Facilitator: Ask, "how did it go"? and get everyone involved in the discussion. Announce the theme for the next session, "Seeing Through Other's Eyes/ I's." Since the next session will be the last discussion for the set what do we want to do? Will we have extra time and refreshments or an extra session for socializing and/or dinner?

Make sure everyone can agree on these questions and clarify what happens. Then confirm the date and place for session 7. Who hosts, facilitates and brings refreshments?

Closing Options (2–4 Minutes)

Reading of Sunday scripture or other options your group has become accustomed to.

Refreshments (1/2 hour)

YEAR 3 - W - 7

Theme: Seeing Through Other's Eyes / I's

Gathering Time—Welcoming and Sharing (15–20 Minutes)

Facilitator: Make sure that the hosting and

hospitality go well. Announce the theme. Ask someone to read the following after the focus exercise.

Focus Exercise (2–3 Minutes)

Learning Reflection

We have to see things from different points of view to see what's really there. For example, you see the back of a person's head and think you know the person. But looking from another angle, you realize it is not the person you thought. (Pause for 2–3 minutes of reflection)

Small Discussion Group (15–20 Minutes)

Facilitator: Ask the people to divide into groups of three or two if necessary and discuss the following questions.

1. Talk about a time when you had an experience that you interpreted one way, but when you got other people's perspectives, you changed your mind.

2. When making a decision or discerning, who do you normally choose to listen to? Why?

3. Do you seek out other points of view or just reinforce (by what you read, who you talk to, etc.) what you already accept?

Large Group Discussion (30 Minutes)

Facilitator: Gather the people again into one large group and facilitate dialogue about the following questions. Give the people a minute warning to finish their discussions and then ask them to discuss the final question. Just before that discussion have someone read the lines for reflection.

1. Tell about a time when you deliberately tuned out another point of view

that prevented you from seeing from another perspective. What were the circumstances?

2. What are some blocks that consistently keep you from hearing others' perspectives?

3. What people have you chosen for role models, both socially and spiritually?

4. How can you learn to perceive other points of view better? For example, reading materials with a variety of viewpoints.

Learning Reflection

In our church perspective, God creates us and calls us as a people. That's why the communion of saints is so important. God's revelation comes and continues to come through the communion of saints.

5. How has this small group been an experience of the communion of saints for you?

Wrap-up and Evaluation (10 Minutes)

Facilitator: Since this is the last discussion for this set ask someone to take notes. Also, the parish might want a report from the group. Facilitate a discussion of the whole set of sessions. What went well, what would we like to improve? This may be a general discussion but try to be as specific as possible.

Closing Options (4–5 Minutes)

Facilitator: Since this is the last session you may want scripture readings to be followed by a short prayer time. Be sure that this is something that everyone can feel comfortable with.

Refreshments or Special Celebration

YEAR 3 - S - 1

Theme: Celebrations—Interconnections

Gathering Time—Welcoming and Sharing (20 Minutes)

Facilitator: Make sure that hospitality and welcoming goes well. Everyone should be greeted at the door and begin to catch up since the last time. Announce the theme for the session. Ask someone to do the reading after the focus exercise.

Focus Exercise (2–3 Minutes)

Large Group Discussion (20 Minutes)

Facilitator: Facilitate the whole group dialogue about the following questions.

1. Did you have any celebrations since we last met? Who was there? What did you do?
2. Other than a "pity party," what kind of party do you have by yourself? Can you give an example?

Small Group Discussion (20–25 Minutes)

Facilitator: Ask the group to break into small groups of three for discussing the following questions.

1. Why was it important for the people who were at your celebrations (that you talked about in the large group) to be there?
2. What happened that could not have happened if you were alone?
3. Does it make a difference who you celebrate with? How do you choose who you celebrate with?

Large Group Discussion (20 Minutes)

Facilitator: Ask people to come together in a large group and lead a conversation about the way interconnections are shown or experienced at celebrations of mass.

Wrap-up and Evaluation (3–5 Minutes)

Facilitator: Spend some time asking people how the session went. Did anyone have any problems picking up again in the large group? Was there anything that we should do differently? Announce the theme for the next session, "Celebrations—Sacred/Secular." Confirm all the details for next time: date, time, place, direction. Who will facilitate, host and bring refreshments?

Closing Options (2–4 Minutes)

Facilitator: Reading of Sunday scripture is always good but the group will begin to settle into some form of prayer routine that is comfortable for all. This may take different forms but it should always be respectful of all the members of the group.

Refreshments (1/2 hour)

Enjoy! Simple! Socializing!

YEAR 3 - S - 2

Theme: Celebrations—Sacred/Secular

Gathering Time—Welcoming and Sharing (15–20 Minutes)

Facilitator: As usual make sure that the welcoming and hospitality go well and that everyone gets a time to chat about their day. As they are seated announce the theme of the session. It would be good to read a section of the Guidelines for Sharing that you think might be helpful. Be prepared to read the thoughts for reflection and discussion later on.

Focus Exercise (2–3 Minutes)

Large Group Discussion (20–30 Minutes)

Facilitator: Facilitate a discussion of the whole group about the following questions.

1. Name some sacred and secular celebrations you have participated in, and briefly tell something about each one. (Allow sufficient time for each person to contribute.)

2. What effect did each of these celebrations have on you or someone close to you?

3. In what ways do they—the sacred and secular—differ from each other? Be specific.

Learning Reflection

Most of our festivals came from pagan roots. For example, the nativity was celebrated on a variety of dates until it was connected to the winter solstice celebration. The pagans didn't distinguish between the sacred and secular. For them everything was controlled by the gods of good and the gods of evil.
(Pause for a few moments)

Small Group Discussion (30 Minutes)

Facilitator: Ask people to break into groups of three and discuss the following questions.

1. Give an example of a secular celebration. Does it have any sacred aspects?

2. Give an example of a sacred celebration. Can you name any secular aspects of the celebration?

3. Is there a difference in the ways you are touched by each of these celebrations? Describe.

4. Can you tell about a time when you experienced the sacred in the ordinary events of your life? What habits do we need to develop to do this on a daily basis?

Wrap-up and Evaluation (3–5 Minutes)

Facilitator: Ask for feedback from everyone as to how the session went. Are we all entering into speaking and listening? Announce that the next session will be a do-it-yourself session and the theme will be "Conflict." Confirm all the details for the next meeting, especially who will facilitate, host and bring refreshments.

Closing Options (2–4 Minutes)

Readings from scripture or prayers that your group finds satisfactory.

Refreshments (1/2 hour)

Enjoy and socialize!

YEAR 3 - S - 3

Theme: Conflict

Gathering Time—Welcoming and Sharing (15–20 Minutes)

Facilitator: Hospitality will happen if everyone is responsible. You will have to provide an easel or space on a wall for writing on newsprint. Remember to always use a double sheet of newsprint so that no ink will go through to the wall. Also supply newsprint (a roll from a press is much cheaper) and a felt pen. Some masking tape will be needed. Scotch tape sticks harder to walls. As people are being seated announce that this is a do-it-yourself session. Therefore the group will remain together as a whole group the entire time.

Focus Exercise (2–3 Minutes)

Learning Reflection

The session will focus on our experience of human conflict and conflict resolution. Conflict is a part of every healthy relationship. Conflict that is avoided eventually poisons a relationship. The same is true for groups. If a group expects to grow in a healthy manner, the group must eventually deal with conflict. Conflict resolution is not an innate ability but a skill that can be developed. Small conflicts often begin with differing expectations.

Values are priorities that underlie the specific behaviors or desires that lead to conflict. We will be examining values in both sides of a real conflict.

Small Group Discussion (10 Minutes)

Facilitator: Ask the people to divide into groups of three and talk about the following question.

1. Has our group gone beyond the honeymoon stage and experienced conflict? Name, but don't solve, a present conflict that is spoken or unspoken within the group.

Large Group Discussion (50 Minutes)

Facilitator: Ask each group to present the conflicts they discussed. Use a sheet of newsprint for each conflict presented. Take your time but make sure that each conflict is written down so that all can see. Then begin a discussion of the following questions.

1. Ask one person to state one side of the

conflict and another to summarize the other side of the conflict.

2. Drawing on values talked about in previous sessions, name the values that underlie each side in the conflict. (See the table of contents for the titles of the sessions to help remember the values discussed.) List the values in two columns on the newsprint for each side of the conflict.

3. Prioritize the values listed, for example, one side might be #1 Belonging, #2 Equality, #3 Self-confidence; and the other side might be #1 Valuing Self, #2 Service and #3 Belonging.

4. Considering each side of the conflict separately, can we make a list of alternate behaviors that would keep the same values on each side, and also take into account the values of the opposite side?

5. Finally, can we find a behavior for the group that retains the values of each column? (Write it on the newsprint.) Does it fit the group? Do we need to think more about it? (The answer may not necessarily come now.)

Wrap-up and Evaluation (5–10 Minutes)

Facilitator: Ask everyone to evaluate the session. What was the quality of listening? Has the group negotiated a conflict in the past? Does our experience from this session say something about our future together? Make sure everyone gets a chance to say something. Announce the theme for the next session, "Common Sense/Common Wisdom." Confirm the details of the next meeting. Who brings refreshments, hosts, facilitates?

Closing Options (2–4 Minutes)

Facilitator: This would be a good time to have a very comfortable form of prayer and or scripture reading since there may have been some emotions stirring during the discussions.

Refreshments (1/2 hour)

Enjoy! Relax and socialize.

YEAR 3 - S - 4

Theme: Common Sense/Common Wisdom

Gathering Time—Welcoming and Sharing (15–20 Minutes)

Facilitator: The hospitality will probably be a habit with everyone by now. However, you are the co-leader for this session to make sure all is well. As people are seated announce the theme. You might want to read a section of the Guidelines for Sharing if something is appropriate.

Focus Exercise (2–3 Minutes)

Small Group Discussion (15 Minutes)

Facilitator: Ask people to divide into groups of three for discussion of the following question.

1. What is the difference between common *sense* and common prejudice? Has there been a time when you experienced one or the other?

Large Group Discussion (45 Minutes)

Facilitator: Ask the people to gather again into one large group. Read the following definitions and after a few moments pause facilitate a discussion by the whole group of the questions that follow the definitions.

COMMON SENSE—Good sound ordinary sense; good judgment or prudence in estimating or managing affairs, especially as not dependent on special or technical knowledge or intellectual subtlety

COMMON—Relating to a group (community) at large; known to the community; belonging to or typical to all people

SENSE—Sensation, feeling, understanding, signification; something to be grasped, to be comprehended (Synonyms: good sense, horse sense, judgment, wisdom, gumption)

WISDOM—Accumulated information; intelligent application of learning; the ability to discern inner qualities and essential relationships

PREJUDICE—Previous judgment, precedent, detriment; an injury or damage due to some judgment or action of another; preconceived judgment or opinion without grounds or before sufficient knowledge; an opinion or judgment formed beforehand or without due examination

For Discussion

1. What is your understanding of common sense? Tell of a time when you experienced it.
2. Who has been a role model of common wisdom, common sense for you, how and why?
3. What is your understanding of common prejudice? Tell of a time when you experienced it.

Wrap-up and Evaluation (4–5 Minutes)

Facilitator: Spend some time reviewing how the session went. Did everyone get a chance to talk? Announce the theme for the next session, "Common Cause/Common Good." Confirm the details for next time, who hosts, brings refreshments, facilitates.

Closing Options (2–4 Minutes)

Facilitator: We highly recommend reading one or more of the readings from the coming Sunday mass.

Refreshments (1/2 hour)

YEAR 3 - S - 5

Theme: Common Cause/Common Good

Gathering Time—Welcoming and Sharing (15–20 Minutes)

Facilitator: Everyone is now used to being co-responsible for this time. Announce the theme for the session. If reading part of the Guidelines for Sharing would be profitable do it. After the focus exercise read the thought for discussion.

Focus Exercise (2–3 Minutes)

This may have become routine by now but don't let it become a rut.

Learning Reflection

The key to our individual good and our common good follows from getting basic needs met. Personal basic needs are met better within a small group rather than alone or in a large group.

Small Group Discussion (35–40 Minutes)

Facilitator: Ask the people to divide into small groups for discussing the following questions.

1. Over the past three years, what are some of the key basic values that you have experienced or discussed in this group?
2. Talk about some specific times you have felt affirmed by this group.
3. Talk about the different groups you belong to. Do you help others to feel they also belong? Describe in what ways.
4. Talk about how you feel liked or disliked by others, in this and other groups. Do you like others in the groups you are a part of? If so, do you express it in some way?
5. Do you feel you can speak freely in this group? Why or why not? Is this the same in other groups? What are some differences?

Large Group Discussion (20–25 Minutes)

Facilitator: Ask people to come back together as a large group and discuss the following questions.

1. When and how have you helped another person in another group experience feeling affirmed? Feeling they really belong? Feeling they are liked?
2. Describe experiences in other groups you belong to that have helped you feel worthwhile and affirmed.
3. Has this group built up any traditions? If so, describe.

Wrap-up and Evaluation (4–5 Minutes)

Facilitator: With the group, review the session. What do we think about it? Did we all contribute? (Notice we do not say do we all agree.) Is there learning? Announce the theme for the next session, "Life for Now/Vocation." Confirm the details, date, time, place and especially who will bring refreshments, host and facilitate.

Closing Options (2–4 Minutes)

A prayer or scripture reading

Refreshments (1/2 hour)

YEAR 3 - S - 6

Theme: Life for Now/Vocation

Gathering Time—Welcoming and Sharing (15–20 Minutes)

Facilitator: The hospitality should be dynamic with everyone involved. Announce the theme for the week.

Focus Exercise (2–3 Minutes)

Large Group Discussion (60 Minutes)

Facilitator: This is an unusual session in that it is all large group. Make sure that everyone will be concerned that each person be given an opportunity to be heard about each question. These should be revelations of each person's life experiences. Remember, it is not important to get through all the questions, but rather to have a good dialogue. No one person dominates or no person is left out.

1. What are some of things you have learned over the last three years?
2. Tell a story about what you have learned about discipline.
3. Give an example of something that you have you learned about yourself, your life, and about the life of Jesus?

4. What have you learned about Catholic tradition?
5. How has being a part of this group helped you to become more whole, holy, Catholic, apostolic?
6. Tell a story about what have you learned about common worship, prayer, spirituality.
7. What do you see as your vocation? What is *our* vocation?

Vocation is what I'm focusing on now not sometime in the future.

8. Do you have any feedback for other members of the group on how you see their vocation?

Wrap-up and Evaluation (5–6 Minutes)

Facilitator: How was the different format? Did we learn how to participate in a larger group, since this is often the situation in much of our life? Announce the theme for next time, "Life Forever—Endless Summer." Should we have a special celebration since next time is the last for us this year? Confirm all the details about the celebration and next time, if they are separate or together.

Closing Options (2–3 Minutes)

Refreshments (1/2 hour)

Enjoy and socialize!

YEAR 3 - S - 7

Theme: Life Forever—Endless Summer

Gathering Time—Welcoming and Sharing (15–20 Minutes)

Facilitator: Hospitality will be easily done

at this point. Make sure everyone is talking about the day, or important happenings. Announce the theme for this last session of this year. Again we will not be breaking into smaller groups. After the focusing exercise read the reading.

Focus Exercise (2–3 Minutes)

Learning Reflection

Hope is faith in a positive future. Wishful thinking is not hope. People don't live in "endless summer"—we experience special moments when time seems to stand still, then we return to ordinary time. In these peak moments we seem to touch eternity—a glimpse of what will be. The temptation is to want to stay with the peak moment. The reality is we touch it briefly but it energizes us to return to ordinary time.

Large Group Discussion (60 Minutes)

Facilitator: Facilitate a dialogue about the following questions, making sure that no one dominates and that all have a chance to say something about every question.

1. Tell about a time when you have felt completely happy, when time seemed to stand still. What made it special?
2. Tell what gets you excited or gives you energy.
3. What gives you hope?
4. What are the differences between questions 2 and 3? (reread)

Wrap-up and Evaluation (5–10 Minutes)

Facilitator: Spend time reviewing the session, how did it go? Are there any special comments, since this is our last session for the year?

Closing Options (4-5 Minutes)

Facilitator: This might be a little longer prayer time, yet comfortable for all.

Refreshments (1/2 hour)

Enjoy and socialize!

CHAPTER 7

YEAR 4 - F - 1

Theme: Patriotism and Loyalty

Gathering Time—Welcoming and Introductions (20 Minutes)

Facilitator: Make sure the usual hospitality is done well and everyone is involved. Announce the theme for the session. This is a big year. Looking ahead we see that this set has three do-it-yourself sessions. We have become accustomed to the process, and we are now going to be asked to create it ourselves. So that we can be a little more aware as we go along, you may want to refer to the do-it-yourself How to Plan Your Own Sessions in chapter 3.

Focus Exercise (2–3 Minutes)

Small Group Discussion (25–30 Minutes)

Facilitator: Ask the people to divide into small groups (three is always a good size here) and dialogue about the following questions.

1. Give some examples of times when you have been proud to be an American, to be a Catholic.
2. Relate experiences when you have *not* been proud to be an American or a Catholic.
3. How do you express loyalty—for a friend, for your country, for your church?

4. Do you fulfill your promises, stated or unstated, in your relationships?
5. Tell of a time when you've been supportive of someone's national pride.

Large Group Discussion (30–35 Minutes)

Facilitator: Ask the members to return to a large group and discuss the following questions.

1. How do you feel when others do not keep their promises?
2. How do you show or not show loyalty to others, to our small group?
3. How does our small group show or not show loyalty to our parish?

Wrap-up and Evaluation (5–7 Minutes)

Facilitator: Spend some time critiquing the session. How did the group pick up after not meeting for some time? Is there anything anyone wants to say before we end?

We have to decide on the theme for next week, so ask everyone to look in Appendix A for some value that would serve as our focal point. You might want to brainstorm for a couple of minutes now. Keep the ideas in mind for next week. Confirm the details for the next meeting; time, place, date, who brings refreshments, hosts, facilitates.

Closing Options (2–4 Minutes)

Refreshments (1/2 hour)

Enjoy and socialize.

YEAR 4 - F - 2

Theme: Whatever You Chose Last Time

Gathering Time—Welcoming and Sharing (15–20 Minutes)

Facilitator: You need to supply paper, pencils, newsprint, marker and masking tape so that the group can proceed to plan and do this session. You can keep the format of previous sessions. In fact, there have been several different formats used, although there is a general outline. The whole point is to keep everyone involved in speaking and listening about personal experiences of group members as they pertain to the chosen theme. Continue to practice the art of question writing, and then dialoguing about them. You may want to refer to How to Plan Your Own Sessions in chapter 3.

Every week make sure the details for the next meeting are taken care of before the session ends. This includes the theme, given or chosen, the kind of session it is and all the physical details, who facilitates, hosts and brings refreshments.

YEAR 4 - F - 3

Theme: Personal Prayer

Gathering Time—Welcoming and Sharing (20 Minutes)

Facilitator: As the hospitality, greeting and mingling go on make sure that everyone is co-responsible. Announce the theme for the session. Ask someone to do the reading later.

Focus Exercise (2–3 Minutes)

A Reading from *With Open Hands* by Henri Nouwen

Someone will tell you, "You have to be able to forgive yourself." But that isn't possible. What is possible is to open your hands without fear, so the other can blow your sins away. For perhaps it isn't clammy coins, but just a light dust which a soft breeze will whirl away, leaving only a grin or a chuckle behind. Then you feel a bit of new freedom, and praying becomes a joy, a spontaneous reaction to the world and the people around you. Praying becomes effortless, inspired and lively, or peaceful and quiet. Then you recognize the festive and the modest as moments of prayer. You begin to suspect that to pray is to live.
(Pause for a few moments)

Small Group Discussion (20 Minutes)

Facilitator: Ask the people to divide into small groups and talk about the following questions.

1. When you pray, is it about the past, the present or the future? Give examples.
2. When you pray is it to ask for favors, to give thanks?
3. What is the difference between being with God in silence, talking with God, and using standardized prayers? Tell some specific experiences of these.

Large Group Discussion (40 Minutes)

Facilitator: Ask the people to gather into one group and dialogue about the following questions.

1. When you pray do you have certain formal prayers or prayer books, the Bible, etc., that you use?
2. In talking about question 3 in your small groups, what were some stories or comments that seemed significant to you?

3. Can you describe a time when you had real difficulty in praying? What was it like and what did you do?

4. Describe a time when you felt very prayerful, when you felt God's presence.

5. Are there types of prayer that you've heard about that you would like to know about? Do you have resources that you could share with the group?

Wrap-up and Evaluation (5–7 Minutes)

Facilitator: Ask for comments from everyone. How did the session go? Announce that next week will be a do-it-yourself session. Again, what do we want the topic to be? You can decide in your own words or look in Appendix A. Confirm all the details and plans for the next session.

Closing Options (2–4 Minutes)

Refreshments (1/2 hour)

YEAR 4 - F - 4

Theme: Whatever You Decided It Should Be

Gathering Time—Welcoming and Sharing

By now the process has probably become habit. It is important that there be a structured plan followed. Otherwise over time it degenerates into personal agendas and the energy will eventually slacken.

Structured dialogue about specific topics involving life experiences is different than a session that "just came together at the last moment." If we are to stay productive it takes time, work, discipline. All

these things are the essence of the spiritual life. But then that is what this process has promoted.

There are an infinite variety of topics, resources of spiritual reading, scripture. Daily life is full of experiences and values that need to be shared in the light of faith, tradition and scripture. So on with the process

As each meeting concludes confirm all the details for the next time: place, date, time, theme, who hosts, facilitates, and brings refreshments.

YEAR 4 - F - 5

Theme: Reconciliation

Gathering Time—Welcoming and Sharing (15–20 Minutes)

Facilitator: Make sure that all is in place for everyone to participate. The facilitator is a real service position for the evening. This time have paper and pencils. Announce that this will be another do-it-yourself session. It is always good to review the guidelines for sharing at least once every set of sessions. You can read the Session Development section or ask someone else to do it.

Focus Exercise (2–3 Minutes)

Session Development

In the first half of this session we will work in pairs to develop a set of four questions we could raise to stimulate a discussion of reconciliation in our lives as Christians. Reconciliation is a New Testament topic. It does not appear in the Old Testament. It appears in many forms in our lives as Catholics and touches on many associated realities: sin, guilt, confession, forgiveness, absolution, penance. These may come up in our discussion, but our main focus will be on the human theme of overcoming separation and repairing ruptures in our relationships. Relationships between ourselves and one another, between ourselves and a community, between ourselves and God.

Reconciliation Involves:

1. Giving positive mental assent to the reality that one has boundaries and inabilities and that one's limits are the framework for exercising one's talents and making one's unique contribution.
2. The ability to laugh at one's own imperfections, as well as rejoice in one's gifts and strengths.
3. Recognizing the boundaries and limitations of another person and seeing them as a framework for exercising their talents and making their unique contribution.
4. Healing a rupture and bringing the parties back together into a renewed and graceful relationship.
5. Ending of separation, removal of barriers, and restoration of relationship through affirmation of appropriate boundaries. (The colloquial term for this is "fence-mending.") Neither party should be absorbed into the other. Reconciliation rejoices in the true freedom and uniqueness of each person.

Small Group Writing (20 Minutes)

Facilitator: Ask the people to break up into small groups and read the instructions and definitions. Then come up with three question for another group to discuss and one for the whole group to talk about. Remember to keep the questions focused on personal experience.

Small Group Discussion (20 Minutes)

Facilitator: Ask the groups to exchange questions and talk about the ones they receive.

Large Group Discussion (20 Minutes)

Facilitator: Ask the people to gather into one group and discuss the one question that each group wrote for them.

Wrap-up and Evaluation (5–7 Minutes)

Facilitator: Have the group critique the session. How did we do? Announce that the next session will be totally do-it-yourself. So what do we want the theme to be so it can be in the back of our minds this week? Remember, someone might have a short quote that would fit and get our thoughts focused, although the questions will always be about our personal experience. Confirm all the details for the next session, including date, place, time, theme; who facilitates, hosts and brings refreshments.

Closing Options (2–4 Minutes)

Refreshments (1/2 hour)

YEAR 4 - F - 6

Theme: Whatever You Have Decided

This is another learning opportunity to develop your own process. This is the first part of the rest of your lives. Many of the sessions of the past have had too many questions. You might go back to that topic and talk about the questions you didn't get to before. Also all the questions probably will evoke different responses now than they did then. This is another alternative.

Since the next session will be your last now is the time to plan ahead for some special celebration as this set comes to a close and the holidays are near.

Make sure to plan and confirm all the details for the next meeting before closing this one.

YEAR 4 - F - 7

Theme: Enfleshment/Incarnation

Gathering Time—Welcoming and Sharing (20 Minutes)

Facilitator: Make sure it all happens and everyone is involved and comfortable. Announce the theme for the session. Ask someone to read the reflection later.

Focus Exercise (2–3 Minutes)

A Reading from *Seeds of Contemplation* by Thomas Merton

Spiritual life is not a mental life: it is not thought alone. Nor is it, of course, a life of sensation, a life of feeling…alone….Nor does the spiritual life exclude thought and feeling. It needs both…if a [person] is to live, he must be all alive, body, soul, mind, heart, spirit. (Brief Pause)

A Reading from Philippians 2:3–8

Never act out of rivalry or conceit; rather, let all parties think humbly of others as superior to themselves, each of you looking to others'

interests rather than their own. Your attitude must be that of Christ: Though he was in the form of God, he did not deem equality with God something to be grasped at. Rather he emptied himself and took the form of a slave, being born in the likeness of men.

He was known to be of human estate, and it was thus that he humbled himself, obediently accepting even death, death on a cross! (Pause for a few moments)

Small Group Discussion (25 Minutes)

Facilitator: Ask the people to break into small groups and talk about the following questions.

1. How do you prepare for Christmas?
2. How do you experience Christmas, both the spiritual and the secular?
3. What are your expectations for how you should experience Christmas?
4. What are the blocks, limitations, that keep you from celebrating Christmas as you wish? How do you let go or not let go?
5. How is Christmas an experience of limitations and letting go?

Large Group Discussion (35 Minutes)

Facilitator: Ask the group to reassemble and discuss the following questions. If there is time you could go back to some of the small group questions.

1. What are some ways you can celebrate Christmas more realistically?
2. Do your expectations get in the way of more fully experiencing Christmas?

Wrap-up and Evaluation (5–7 Minutes)

Facilitator: Ask everyone to review the session. How did it go? Confirm details for meeting for the next set of sessions after the holidays. People will probably want names, addresses and phone numbers if that was not already available. Continue with your special celebration or do that at another time.

Closing Options (4–5 Minutes)

This would be a good time for a slightly more extended prayer time.

Refreshments (1/2 hour)

Merry Christmas!

YEAR 4 - W - 1

Theme: Reunion—Rebelonging—Realizing

This is a good place to try your hand at some of these things. When the group is gathering after a period of absence this kind of need is present. See what you can do with it. See Appendix A for theme suggestions and How to Plan Your Own Sessions in chapter 3 if you want reminders. It might be a good idea to confirm all the dates for this set of sessions at this time. Specifically plan the details for the next session.

YEAR 4 - W - 2

Theme: Reconciliation—Mine/Ours

Gathering Time—Welcoming and Sharing (10–15 Minutes)

Facilitator: Help greet and welcome everyone. Announce the theme for the session. This will be about each of our needs and our collective need to forgive. Ask someone to do the reading.

Focus Exercise (2–3 Minutes)

A Reading from *Making Friends with Yourself* by Leo Rock, S.J.

Jesus said this: "If you bring your gift to the altar, and there recall that your brother or sister has anything against you, leave your gift there at the altar, go first to be reconciled with your brother or sister, and then come and offer your gift." (Mt 5:23–24) If this is true for reconciliation between us and a brother or sister, how much more true is it for reconciliation with our inner selves? If we would seek reconciliation with God and others, don't we first have to seek to be reconciled with ourselves? The cure is, indeed, expensive, but not beyond our means. The cure does take time, but that's what time is for. Saints are living proof of the curability of the malady. For all of their immense differences from one another, saints have one thing in common: they let God love them, and so heal them.

Small Group Discussion (30 Minutes)

Facilitator: Ask the people to break into groups of three and talk about the following questions.

1. When have you forgiven someone else?
2. What was the occasion? Did they ask for forgiveness or admit wrongdoing? Did you get tired of waiting for them to ask? Were interaction and words involved in forgiveness?
3. How do you know when you need reconciliation?
4. Tell of an experience when you wronged another person or someone had a grievance against you. When you have been wronged, how do you respond?
5. Have you ever had an experience when someone did not forgive you?

Has there been a time when you did not forgive someone—if so, share only if you feel comfortable?

6. Have you ever asked someone to help in reconciliation? How did it work out? Share only in general if that is preferable.

Large Group Discussion (25 Minutes)

Facilitator: Gather the groups into one and ask them to discuss the following questions.

1. When have you been involved in a situation within a group, when the group needed to ask for forgiveness?
2. In what ways are you responsible for the actions of a group you belong to?
3. Are there whole groups of people you find difficult to forgive?
4. How does your perspective influence your understanding of reconciliation?

Wrap-up and Evaluation (3–5 Minutes)

Facilitator: Encourage the people to review and critique the session. Take care of all the details for the next session, which includes preparing to plan your own.

Closing Options (2–4 Minutes)

Refreshments (1/2 hour)

YEAR 4 - W - 3

Theme: Whatever You Make It

This is a good time to do your own session on welcoming, feeling cared for, belonging, etc. Choose some such topic and revisit that area. You might also do something on getting reconnected. Some earlier topics and questions would be a good starting point.

Always confirm the details for the next meeting before you end.

YEAR 4 - W - 4

Theme: Yours to Decide

Think of the season and what fits. Look at the list in Appendix A for ideas. You'll need to keep some kind of structure.

Make sure everyone is clear about the details for the next meeting.

YEAR 4 - W - 5

Theme: Heroes/Heroines—Role Models and Saints

Gathering Time—Welcoming and Sharing (10–25 Minutes)

Facilitator: Hospitality and greeting are co-responsible efforts for everyone. Announce the theme for the session.

Focus Exercise (2–3 Minutes)

A Reading from *Seeds of Contemplation* by Thomas Merton

Many poets are not poets for the same reason that many Christians are not saints: they never succeed in being themselves. They never get around to being the particular poet or the particular persons they are intended to be by God. They never become the man or woman or artist or poet who is called for by all the circumstances of their individual lives.

They waste their years in vain efforts to be some other poet, some other saint. For many absurd reasons, they are convinced that they are obliged to become somebody else who died two hundred years ago and who lived in circumstances utterly alien to their own.

They wear out their minds and bodies in a hopeless endeavor to have somebody else's experiences or write somebody else's poems or possess somebody else's goodness.

Hurry ruins saints as well as artists. They want quick success, and they are in such a haste to get it that they cannot take time to be true to themselves. And when the madness is upon them they argue that their very haste is a species of integrity.

(Pause for a few moments)

Small Group Discussion (30 Minutes)

Facilitator: Ask the people to divide into small groups and dialogue about the following questions.

1. What do you want to say about these readings? Feelings, reactions?
2. What challenge(s) are there for you in these readings?
3. Tell about one or more of your models, heroes, heroines or saints. Why are they significant for you?

Large Group Discussion (30 Minutes)

Facilitator: Ask everyone to regather into one group for discussion of the following questions.

1. Did anyone name a living person as a hero/heroine, saint in your small groups? Who is it? Do you have difficulty thinking of a living person as a "saint"? If so, why?
2. In what way are you a role model, a hero or heroine to others?

Wrap-up and Evaluation (4–5 Minutes)

Facilitator: After a brief critique talk about the next two sessions which you are plan-

ning. You might divide the group in half and each plan a session. Confirm all the details for the next sessions along with selecting topics for them.

Closing Options (2–4 Minutes)

Facilitator: For a change of pace you might use the following. Divide the group in half.

(1) O Lord, our Lord
   how glorious is your name over
   all the earth
You have exalted your majesty above
   the heavens
Out of the mouths of babes and
   sucklings
      you have fashioned praise
      because of your foes
      to silence the hostile and the
      vengeful.

(2) When I behold your heavens, the
   work of your fingers
      the moon and stars which you set
      in place—
What are we that you should be
   mindful of us
      or our children that you should
      care for them?

(All) You have made us little less than the
   angels
      and crowned us with glory and
      honor.
You have given us rule over the works
   of your hands,
      putting all things under our feet:
All sheep and oxen, yes, and the
   beasts of the field,
The birds of the air, the fishes of the
   sea,

and whatever swims the paths of
the seas.
O Lord, our Lord,
how glorious is your name over
all the earth!

Refreshments (1/2 hour)

YEAR 4 - W - 6

Theme: Your Selection

The theme will have been decided last time along with the details. This time remember to plan for the last session of the year. You will need a theme, all the details of place, etc.

YEAR 4 - W - 7

Theme: Whatever You Decide

This could include a celebration, or that could be a separate event.

YEAR 4 - S - 1

Theme:

You might do something on vacation or play or spontaneity. Remember that it is important to have some structure and a particular topic. How to Plan Your Own Sessions in chapter 3 may be of help, as well as Appendix A.

YEAR 4 - S - 2

Theme:

Again this is your selection.

YEAR 4 - S - 3

Theme: Celebrations—Peons and Popes

Gathering Time—Welcoming and Sharing (15 Minutes)

Facilitator: Help the host to make sure all goes well. Announce the theme after people have become seated.

Focus Exercise (2–3 Minutes)

Learning Reflection

Every culture has systems of hierarchy and systems of equality and we exist simultaneously in both.

Small Group Discussion (30–35 Minutes)

Facilitator: Ask the people to break into small groups and talk about the following questions.

1. Give examples of how you treat those above you—in positions of responsibility at work, at the parish, in the community, school.

2. Give some examples of how you treat those below you in jobs or responsibility, at work, classes, parish, etc.

Large Group Discussion (30–35 Minutes)

Facilitator: Gather the people into one group and facilitate a discussion of the following questions.

1. Did you have trouble answering the questions in the small group?

2. Tell of a time when you participated in an event when you dressed and acted in a hierarchical role.

3. When have you dressed in a way that defied the system? Was it deliberate? How did people react?

4. We often use different words in different ways with different people. Give some examples from your experience.

Wrap-up and Evaluation (4–5 Minutes)

Facilitator: Ask if there is anything someone would like to say before we finish. The next two sessions will be ours to plan. What shall our themes be so we can be thinking about them? Confirm the details about themes and about the next session.

Closing Options (2–4 Minutes)

Refreshments (1/2 hour)

YEAR 4 - S - 4

Theme: Yours to Choose

YEAR 4 - S - 5

Theme: Whatever Is Appropriate for the Group Now

YEAR 4 - S - 6

Theme: Living in the Now—Between the Two Comings

Gathering Time—Welcoming and Sharing (15–20 Minutes)

Facilitator: All that happens should be almost by habit, but make sure it works well. Announce the theme when people are seated. Ask some one to read the short reading later.

Focus Exercise (2–3 Minutes)

Learning Reflection

The Church teaches that Christ is present when even groups of two or three are gathered together in His name. We read in scripture and know from tradition that the people of God assembled privately and publicly in His name. Christ is present in His word when the scripture is read, in the sacraments, especially in the Eucharist and in the person of the anointed minister (priest).

(Pause for a few moments)

Small Discussion Group (30 Minutes)

Facilitator: Break the group into small groups and talk about the following questions.

1. Jesus the Christ came. He will come again. Where is the focus of these statements?

2. If the focus of the two comings is on the distant past and distant future, where is Christ in the present?

3. How is Christ present for you TODAY?

Large Group Discussion (30–35 Minutes)

Facilitator: Gather everyone into one group and discuss the following questions.

1. Referring back to the teaching, which of these ways have I been aware of?

2. In what ways do I pay attention and in what ways am I oblivious?

3. Do I really pay more attention to Christ's presence in the past historically, the future or the here and now?

Wrap-up and Evaluation (4–5 Minutes)

Facilitator: Help the group to come to a finish for the session. The next and final session for this set needs to be planned. What will the theme be? This will be the first session of the rest of your lives!

We also suggest some special celebration because the group has spent four years together. The parish may even want to do some recognition. We also suggest that you consider breaking into two groups, adding members and beginning over again. Each session and set of questions would bring several different responses probably.

Remember that next time will be the last meeting of this year. **Make sure you have made plans to meet starting again in the fall.** Plan all the details for that.

Closing Options (4–5 Minutes)

Plan ahead something special here for next time.

Refreshments (1/2 hour)

YEAR 4 - S - 7

Theme: It's All Yours!!!

EPILOGUE

Now that your use of this book has run its course and you have tried your hands (or wings as the saying goes) it's time to do for yourselves for the rest of your life. And it is always good to go back to the basics every so often. There are times when several people have joined the group, supposing others have left, when it may be good to begin at the beginning again. Each time around the same questions will be answered differently.

The process is the most important thing, or in a paraphrase of a famous political statement **It's the process, stupid**. As you've experienced the process it is the way, the method, the meaning by which transformation takes place. There is no perfect process. There are many variations and we have used several in the exercises of this book. By now the general process should be sort of second nature, and you can vary it according to need, desire, effectiveness. Be careful not to let a specific process become rigid. Similarly, don't let the structure degenerate into a free-flowing meeting. A key to successful process is to have a beginning, a middle and an end, that help people to be comfortable, get energized and accomplish something.

The content for short focusing readings can be, and we think should be, widely varied, as are most lives. The real content is always the specific experiences of the persons in the group. We cannot stress this too much. After five years of group experience using this process within our parish some participants who have enjoyed it still yearn to stay in their heads. We occasionally, even now, hear: *The questions should deal more directly with the meditation, or, it would be nice if the questions flowed from the meditation.*

Sometimes current issues are too hot to handle or need to have more reflection time. Again the main emphasis is personal experience. Principles, traditions, scripture, etc., while good and necessary, are secondary to personal experience.

Structured dialogue about specific topics of personal life experience is different from sessions that "just come together at the last moment," or that follow the particular interest of the leader or presenter. If we are to stay productive it takes time, work, discipline. All these things are the essence of the spiritual life.

May the Spirit be with you and guide you, may the communion of saints surround you and give you courage and assistance. And most of all may you, your group(s), and the church become fully alive.

APPENDIX A

Themes of Human Experience

Basic

Self-Preservation
Wonder/Fear
Safety/Survival
Physical Delight
Curiosity/Nature
Economics/Personal & Family
Territory/Personal Space
Courtesy/Hospitality
Belonging
Care/Nurture
Being Liked

Motivation

Balancing Solitude and Intimacy
Dignity/Justice
Building a New Church
Word/Prophecy
Transcendence
Union with the Divine
Insight
Wisdom
Bringing about New Order

Growth

Achievement/Success
Job/Competence
Competition
Efficiency/Planning
Administration/Control
Institution
Loyalty/Group/Nation/Church
Planning Meaningful Liturgy
Education
Law as Duty/Guide
Service
Actualization/Wholeness
Claiming Personal Authority
Empathy/Generosity

APPENDIX B

Readings from the Tradition

You may want to select some of these passages or portions thereof. In some cases they are short enough to use the entire selection. In other cases they are obviously too long for use in one session.

Julian of Norwich, *Showings* 59

The great mystic Julian contemplates motherhood in God.

Jesus is our true Mother in nature by our first creation, and he is our true Mother in grace by his taking our created nature. All the lovely works and all the sweet loving offices of beloved motherhood are appropriated to the second person, for in him we have this godly will, whole and safe forever, both in nature and in grace, from his own goodness proper to him.

I understand three ways of contemplating motherhood in God. The first is the foundation of our nature's creation; the second is his taking of our nature, where the motherhood of grace begins; the third is the motherhood at work. And in that, by the same grace, everything is penetrated, in length and in breadth, in height and in depth without end; and it is all one love.

John Powell, S.J., *The Secret of Staying in Love*, p.11

The essential sadness of our human family is that very few of us even approach the realization of our full potential. Theoreticians claim the average person accomplishes only 10% of his promise. He sees only 10% of the beauty in the

world around him, hears only 10% of the music and poetry in the universe, smells only a tenth of the world's fragrance, and tastes only a tenth of the deliciousness of being alive. He is only 10% open to his emotions, to tenderness, to wonder and awe. His mind embraces only a small part of the thoughts, reflections and understanding of which he is capable. His heart is only 10% alive with love. He will die without ever having really lived or really loved. To me this is the most frightening of all possibilities. I would really hate to think that you or I might die without having really lived and really loved.

Hildegard of Bingen, in *Silent Voices, Sacred Lives*, p. 149

Hildegard's mystical images in this poem comment eloquently on the holy tension of our life in Christ.

O most beautiful form,
O sweetest fragrance of desirable delights
we sigh for you always in our sorrowful banishment!
When may we see you and remain with you?

But we dwell in the world,
and you dwell in our mind;
we embrace you in our heart
as if we had you here with us.

You, bravest lion, have burst through the heavens.
You have destroyed death, and are building life in the golden city.
Grant us society in that city,
and let us dwell in you...

Saint Augustine, writings on the eucharist, from selected sermons.

That bread which you see on the altar, consecrated by the word of God, is the body of Christ. That chalice, or rather, what the chalice holds, consecrated by the word of God, is the Blood of Christ. If you have received worthily, you are what you have received, for the Apostle says: "The bread is one; we though many, are one body." (1 Cor 10:17). Thus he explained the sacrament of the Lord's table: "The bread is one; we though many, are one body." So by bread you are instructed as to how you ought to cherish unity. (Sermon 227)

Brethren, these things are called sacraments because in them the appearance is one thing but the reality is another. What appears to the senses is one thing. A material object, but what is grasped by the mind is a spiritual grace. If you wish then to grasp the body of Christ hear the words of the Apostle to the faithful: "You are the body of Christ and his members" (1 Cor 12:27). If then you are the body of Christ and his members it is your sacrament that reposes on the altar of the Lord. It is your sacrament which you receive. You answer "Amen" to the words "The body of Christ." Be, then, a member of the body of Christ to verify your "Amen." (Sermon 272)

Be what you see, and receive what you are. (Sermon 272)

Recall what this creation of bread once was: how the earth begot it, the rain nourished it, and ripened it; then human labor brought it through various stages—transporting it to the threshing floor, threshing and winnowing it, storing it, bringing it out, grinding, kneading and baking it until at long last bread is produced.

Think too of your own progress: you were brought into existence from non-existence; you were brought to the Lord's threshing floor by the toil of oxen, i.e., by those preaching the Gospel; you were threshed. When you were on probation as catechumens you were in storage in the granary. You enrolled your names, thereby beginning to be ground by fastings and exorcisms. Afterwards you were brought to the water as in

the kneading process, and thus became unified. You were baked by the heat of the Holy Spirit and you became the bread of the Lord.

You are there on the Lord's table, you are actually present in the chalice. You form this mystery with us: we are united in one, we drink together because we live together. (Sermon 272)

Hildegard of Bingen, in *Silent Voices, Sacred Lives*, pp. 52–53

Perhaps Hildegard's vision of the feminine aspect of Jesus can save us from sentimentality in this season and refocus our faith on the mystery of Christ's humanity.

During the celebration on the even of our Lord's Nativity, around the hour of the divine sacrifice, I entered a trance and saw something like a sun of marvelous brightness in the heaven, and in the middle of the sun the likeness of a virgin whose appearance was exceedingly beautiful in form and desirable to see. She was seated on a throne. Her hair was loosened over her shoulders, and on her head was a crown of the most splendid gold. In her right hand was a golden chalice. She was emerging from the sun which surrounded her on all sides. From the virgin herself emanated a splendor of great brilliance, which seemed at first to fill the place of our dwelling. Then gradually expanding after some period of time, it seemed to fill the whole earth.

Now next to that same sun there appeared a great cloud, extremely dark and horrible to see. When I gazed at the cloud, it rushed abruptly against the sun, darkened it, and cut off its splendor from the earth for some time. I saw this happen very often, moreover, so that the world was by turns darkened by the cloud and illuminated by the sun. Whenever it happened that the cloud approached the sun and obstructed its light from the earth, the virgin who was enthroned within the sun seemed to be weeping copiously, as if grieving greatly because of the darkening of the world. I beheld this vision through that day without interruption, and all the following night, for I remained ever wakeful in prayer.

On the holy day of Christmas, now, when the

solemnities of the masses were being celebrated, I asked the holy angel of God who appeared to me what sort of vision that was and what significance it had. He replied to me concerning that virgin, for I especially desired to know who she was, and he said: "That virgin whom you see is the sacred humanity of the Lord Jesus."

Saint John Chrysostom, *Acta Apostolorum,* Homily 26

The night has not been created that we might sleep the whole time without doing anything. This is witnessed by the artisans, merchants, shopkeepers, and the church of God who rise in the middle of the night. Rise up yourself, and see the choir of stars, the deep silence, the great calm, admire the providence of your Lord. As a result the soul is more pure, larger, and more acute; it is raised up and sanctified. The darkness itself and the great silence can lead to compunction....I speak now to men and to women; kneel down, lament, pray to God that he look favorable upon you. He lets himself be persuaded more easily by nocturnal prayers in which you turn the time of repose into a time of mourning....After such vigils, sleep is comforting.

Issac Thomas Hecker, *The Paulist Vocation*

Man not only has a destiny, but each individual of the race has a special destiny, a definite work to do; and this work is a great, an important, a divine work. For, whatever God appoints is great—great in its purpose, important in its accomplishment, divine in its results.

At the same time that God gave to each soul a definite work to do, and marked out for it a special path in life, which, following faithfully, it will attain to its beatitude. He gave also to the soul the strength, courage, talent, grace, to do the work well; and more, to do it with a certain degree of facility and pleasure.

Can the purposes of God, in the case of particular individuals, be so clearly discovered as that each Christian may be matched, so to say, with the state, whether higher or lower, to which God has called him?

The Church answers this question in the affirma-

tive; that is, with the necessary allowance for human error and weakness. The providential destination of individuals in the kingdom of God can be discovered by certain signs and tokens which reach, abstractly speaking, to the certainity of criteria. The diagnosis of these signs is a main part of the science of Spiritual Direction.

Issac Thomas Hecker, *The Paulist Vocation*

The whole aim of the science of Christian perfection is to instruct men how to remove the hindrances in the way of the action of the Holy Spirit, and how to cultivate those virtues which are most favorable to His solicitations and inspirations. Thus the sum of spiritual life consists in observing and yielding to the movements of the Spirit of God in our soul, employing for this purpose the sacraments, all the exercises of prayer, spiritual reading, the practice of virtues, and good works.

Julian of Norwich, *Showings* 54

The powerful mystical vision of Julian of Norwich gives us fresh words with which to reflect on the mystery of the triune God.

I saw no difference between God and our substance, but as it were, all God; and still my understanding accepted that our substance is in God, that is to say that God is God, and our substance is a creature in God. For the almighty through of the Trinity is our Father, for he made us and keeps us in him. And the deep wisdom of the Trinity is our Mother, in whom we are enclosed. And the high goodness of the Trinity is our Lord, and in him we are enclosed and he is us. We are enclosed in the Father, and we are enclosed in the Son, and we are enclosed in the Holy Spirit. And the Father is enclosed in us, the Son is enclosed in us, and the Holy Spirit is enclosed in us, almighty, all wisdom and all goodness, one God, one Lord.

Saint Bernard, Abbot, *Liturgy of the Hours,* Vol. 3

On the search for wisdom

Let us work for the food which does not perish— our salvation. Let us work in the vineyard of the Lord to earn our daily wage in the wisdom which says: Those who work in me will not sin. Christ tell us: The field is the world. Let us work in it and dig up wisdom, its hidden treasure, a treasure we all look for and want to obtain.

If you look for it, really look. Be converted and come. Converted from what? From your own willfulness. But, you may say, if I do not find wisdom in my own will, where shall I find it? My soul eagerly desires it. And I will not be satisfied when I find it, if it is not a generous amount, a full measure, overflowing into my hands. You are right, for blessed is the man who finds wisdom and is full of prudence.

Look for wisdom while it can still be found. Call for it while it is near. Do you want to know how near it is? The word is near you, in your heart and on your lips, provided that you seek it honestly. Insofar as you find wisdom in your heart, prudence will flow from your lips, but be careful that it flows from and not away from them, or that you do not vomit it up. If you have found wisdom, you have found honey. But do not eat so much that you become full and bring it all up. Eat so that you are always hungry. Wisdom says: Those who eat me continue to hunger. Do not think you have too much of it, but do not eat too much or you will throw it up. If you do, what you seem to have will be taken away from you, because you gave up searching too soon. While wisdom is near and while it can be found, look for it and ask for its help. Solomon says: A man who eats too much honey does himself no good; similarly, the man who seeks his own glorification will be crushed by that same renown.

Happy is the man who has found wisdom. Even more happy is the man who lives in wisdom, for he perceives in abundance. There are three ways for wisdom or prudence to abound in you: If you confess your sins, if you give thanks and praise, and if your speech is edifying. Man believes with his heart and so he is justified. He confesses with his lips and so he is saved. In the beginning of his speech the just man is his own accuser, next he gives glory to God, and thirdly, if his wisdom extends that far he edifies his neighbor.

Saint Catherine of Siena, *Dialogue*

I have ordained every exercise of vocal and mental prayer to bring souls to perfect love for me and their neighbors, and to keep them in this love.

So they offend me more by abandoning charity for their neighbor for a particular exercise or for spiritual quiet than if they had abandoned the exercise for their neighbor. For in charity for their neighbors they find me, but in their own pleasure, where they are seeking me, they will be deprived of me. Why? Because by not helping they are by that very fact diminishing their charity for their neighbors. When their charity for their neighbors is diminished, so is my love for them. And when my love is diminished, so is consolation. So, those who want to gain, lose, and those who are willing to lose, gain. In other words, those who are willing to lose their own consolation for their neighbor's welfare receive and gain me and their neighbors, if they help and serve them lovingly. And so they enjoy the graciousness of my charity at all times.

Saint Gertrude, *Spiritual Exercises*

Carried away one day by the excess of her love, she said to the Lord: "Would, O Lord, that I might have a fire that could liquefy my soul so that I could pour it totally out like a libation unto thee!; The Lord answered: 'Thy will is such a fire.'"

Saint Columban, Abbot, from an instruction, *Liturgy of the Hours*, Vol. 3

God is everywhere in his immensity, and everywhere close at hand. As he says of himself: I am a God close at hand, not a God far off. The God we seek is not one who dwells at a distance from us, for we have him present with us, if only we are worthy. He dwells in us as the soul in the body, if only we are sound members of his, if we are dead to sin. Then in very truth he dwells in us, the one who said: I will dwell in them and walk among them. If we are worthy of his presence with us, then in truth we are made alive by him as his living members. As the Apostle says; In him we live and move and have our being....Seeks then the highest wisdom, not by arguments in words but by the perfection of your life, not by speech but by the faith that comes from simplicity of heart, not from the learned speculations of the unrighteous. If you search by means of discussions for the God who cannot be defined in words, he will depart further from you than he was before. If you search for him by faith, wisdom will stand where wisdom lives, at the gates. Where wisdom is, wisdom will be seen, at least in part. But wisdom is also to some extent truly attained when the invisible God, the object of faith, in a way beyond our understanding for we must believe in God, invisible as he is through is partially seen by a heart that is pure.

Saint Augustine, Bishop, *Liturgy of the Hours*, Vol. 3

Where did I find you, that I came to know you? You were not within my memory, before I learned of you. Where, then, did I find you before I came to know you, if not within yourself, far above me? We come to you and go from you, but no place is involved in this process. In every place, O Truth, you are present to those who seek your help, and at one and the same time you answer all, though they seek your counsel on different matters.

You respond clearly, but not everyone hears clearly. All ask what they wish, but do not always hear the answer they wish. Your best servant is he who is intent not so much on hearing his petition answered, as rather on willing whatever he hears from you.

Late have I loved you, O Beauty ever ancient, ever new, late have I loved you! You were within me, but I was outside, and it was there that I searched for you. In my unloveliness I plunged into the lovely things which you created. You were with me, but I was not with you. Created things kept me from you; yet if they had not been in you they would not have been at all. You called, you shouted, and you broke through my deafness. You flashed, you shone, and you dispelled my blindness. You breathed your fragrance on me; I drew in breath and now I pant for you. I have tasted you; now I hunger and thirst for more. You touched me, and I burned for your peace.

When once I shall be united to you with my whole being, I shall at last be free of sorrow and toil. Then my life will be alive, filled entirely with you. When you fill someone, you relieve him of his burden, but because I am not yet filled with you, I am a burden to myself. My joy when I should be weeping struggles with my sorrows when I should be rejoicing. I know not where victory lies. Woe is me! Lord, have mercy on me! My evil sorrows and good joys are at war with one another. I know not where victory lies. Woe is Me! Lord, have mercy! Woe is me! I make no effort to conceal my wounds. You are my physician, I your patient. You are merciful; I stand in need of mercy.

Aelred of Rievaulx, Abbot, from *The Sexual Celibate* by Donald Goergen

Aelred's discussion of friendship is not simply theory. He basically sees friendship as both a creation of human effort and a gift of God. It is promoted by our own choice and effort as well as by God.

Aelred distinguishes charity, or love, from friendship. Charity is a more inclusive term. "Both enemies and friends are included in the former (love), while to those only to whom we entrust our heart and inmost thought, do we give the name of friend."

True friendship is based on equality, sensitivity and God. "We have still to speak of equality, which is another basic element in friendship. There can be no superior or inferior. Friends should have such understanding as to read at a glance whether the face of the other is overcast with sadness or serene with delight. Are all whom we love in this way to be admitted to the same degree of intimacy? The answer concerns itself with foundations. The house of friendship must be built solidly; therefore, it has need of a firm foundation....The foundation of spiritual friendship is the love of God. Prayer for each other grown more frequent."

Best of all is that the friendship lasts. "Once they

have been made one from two, then since one cannot be divided, so friendship cannot be divided from itself. Hence a friendship that suffers a cleaving of the injured part never was true."

Aelred places a high value on friendship. "Christ himself has given us the length to which friendship should go: 'Greater love than this no one has, that one lay down his life for his friends.' There can be no genuine happiness without a friend. The man who has no one to feel glad of his success or to sympathize with him in sorrow, no one to whom he may pour out the perturbation of his mind, or with whom he may share such luminous thoughts as may come to him, that man can be likened to a beast."

Such friendship does not simply happen. Our choice is involved in who will be admitted to this degree of intimacy. "One is not to receive into friendship all whom he might love, for not all are suited thereto. When a friend enters your life, you so united your life to his as to become, in effect, one from two. You entrust yourself to him as to another self. You neither hide nor fear anything from him." One must be discriminate in his choice since one does not change friendships overnight. Aelred in fact outlines four steps involved in the commitment that friendship implies. Choice was simply the first of these. One should not in boyish fashion change his friends according to caprice. No one is more to be distrusted than he whom has been disloyal to his friends, and nothing disturbs the soul so much as to be forsaken or impugned by a friend. Consequently, there is need of prudence in the choice and of great discrimination in the approval. When once he is admitted, he must be borne with so long as he does not recede irrevocably from the foundation. He is yours, you are his, to the extent of unity of mind, of affection, of will. Four steps there are then to the mound of affection: election, probation, admission, and the highest harmony in matters divine and human joined to affection and good will."

Aelred discussed these four stages. "A friend must first be chosen, then tried, then admitted and thereafter treated as a friend." There are certain people who are excluded in the first stage

from the possibility of being friends. "In the election, we excluded the wrathful, the unstable, the suspicious, and the garrulous: not all, but those who were unwilling to order their passions." After someone is chosen as a possible friend, the test comes as to whether he can really be the deep companion of which Aelred speaks. "We shall next consider probation. The friend must be tested in four things: faith, intention, discretion, and patience." The person is then admitted to the stage of friendship and the highest possible intimacy and harmony follow.

There are certain things which are destructive of friendship and Aelred discusses these. When these are present, they prevent friendship from passing through the first stages or they are reason for dissolving the friendship. Such things are disclosing confidences, jealousy and suspiciousness. Aelred is a real enemy of disclosing the secrets of a friend. "To reveal the confidences of our friends is regarded as sacrilegious." If we are in positions of authority and our friends complain about not receiving some position," Aelred comments, "the one inclined to complain of not being promoted to positions of responsibility would do well to ponder the choice of Peter over John. The fact that Our Lord gave primacy to Peter did not lessen his affection for John." If it ever happens that a relationship has to be dissolved, this must be done carefully. "The friendship is not to be crushed at once, but is gradually to be dissolved, so that no one is hurt."

Saint Augustine, *Confessions* 1–6

But what is it that I love when I love you? Not the beauty of any bodily things, not the order of seasons, not the brightness of light that rejoices the eye, nor the sweet melodies of all songs, nor the sweet fragrance of flowers and ointments and spices; not manna nor honey, not the limbs that carnal love embraces. None of these things do I love in loving my God. Yet in a sense I do love light and melody and fragrance and food and embrace when I love my God—the light and the voice and the fragrance and the food embrace in the soul, when that light shines upon my soul which no place can contain, that voice sounds which no time can take from me, I breathe that fragrance which no wind scatters, I eat the food which is not lessened by the eating, and I lie in the embrace which satiety never comes to sunder. This it is that I love, when\I love my God. And what is this God? I asked the earth and it answered: I am not He, and all things that are in the earth made the same confession. I asked the sea and the deeps and the creeping things, and they answered, We are not our God; seek higher. I asked the winds that blow, and the whole air with all that is in it answered, Anaximines was wrong; I am not God. I asked the heaven, the sun, the moon, the stars, and they answered: Neither are we God whom you seek. And I said to all the things that throng about the gateways of the senses: Tell me of my God, since you are not He. Tell me something of Him. And they cried out in a great voice: He made us. My question was gazing upon them, and their answer was their beauty.

St. Francis, A reflection on the glories of nature, *Praying with St. Francis of Assisi*

Praised be thou, my Lord, with all your
    creatures,
especially Sir Brother Sun,
What is the day and through whom You give us
    light.
And he is beautiful and radiant with great
    splendor;
and bears a likeness of you, Most High One.
Praised be You, my Lord, through Sister Moon
    and the stars,
in heaven You formed them clear and precious
    and beautiful.
Praised be You, my Lord, through Brother Wind,
and through the air, cloudy and serene, and
    every kind of weather
through which You give sustenance to Your
    creatures.
Praised be You, my Lord, through Sister Water,
which is very useful and humble and precious
    and chaste.
Praised be You, my Lord, through Brother Fire,
through whom you light the night
and he is beautiful and playful and robust and
    strong.

Praised be you, my Lord, through our sister
Mother Earth,
who sustains and governs us,
and who produces varied fruits with colored
    flowers and herbs.

Saint John of the Cross, Trusting in God, *Praying with John of the Cross*

In a letter written to a woman who was experiencing spiritual darkness and emptiness, and who felt that God had abandoned her.

While you are in darkness and emptiness of spiritual poverty, you think that everyone and everything are failing you. This is not surprising, for then it also seems to you that God is failing you too. But nothing is wanting to you, nor have you any need to consult me about anything, nor have you reason to do so; for all is merely suspicion without a cause. He who does not want any other thing than God does not walk in darkness, however dark and poor he finds himself....You are in a good way. Be quiet and rejoice. Who are you to be anxious over yourself? You would do well to stop....

Be glad and trust God, who has given you signs that you can very well do so [survive in the darkness] and ought to do so; and if you do not, it will not be surprising that [God] is taking you where it is best for you and has put you in so safe a place. Do not seek for any way but this and calm your soul, for all is well.

Saint Clare, *Praying with Clare of Assisi*

Happy, indeed, is she
    to whom it is given to share in this sacred
      banquet
    so that she might cling with all her heart to
      Him.
        Whose beauty all the blessed hosts of
          heaven
          unceasingly admire,
        Whose affection excites,
        Whose contemplation refreshes,
        Whose kindness fulfills,
        Whose delight replenishes,
        Whose remembrance delightfully shines,
        By Whose fragrance the dead are revived,

Whose glorious vision will bless
all citizens of the heavenly Jerusalem:
which, *since it is the splendor of
eternal glory*, is
*the brilliance of eternal light
and the mirror without blemish.*

Hildegard of Bingen, Moderation and Wellness, *Praying with Hildegard of Bingen*

In a true vision I saw and heard the following words:

O Daughter of God, out of your love for God you call a poor creature like myself, "Mother." Listen, then, to your mother and learn moderation! For moderation is the mother of all the virtues for everything heavenly and earthly. For it is through moderation that the body is nourished with the proper discipline. Any human being who thinks about her sins with sighs of regret—all those sins which she has committed in thought, word, and deed through the Devil's inspiration—must embrace this mother, discretion, and with the counsel of her religious superiors repent of her sins in true humility and sincere obedience. When there are unseasonable downpours, the fruit and vegetables growing on Earth are damaged: when a field has not been plowed, you do not find good grain springing up; instead, there are only useless weeds. It's the same with a person who lays on herself more strain than her body can endure. This is a sign that the effects of holy discretion are weak in such a person. And all of this immoderate straining and abstinence bring nothing useful to such a soul.

Saint Elizabeth Ann Seton, Prayer without Ceasing, *Praying with Elizabeth Seton*

We must pray literally without ceasing—without ceasing; in every occurrence and employment of our lives. You know I mean that prayer of the heart which is independent of place or situation, or which is, rather, a habit of lifting up the heart of God, as in a constant communication with Him.

Julian of Norwich, We Are a Sensual People, *Praying with Julian of Norwich*

And when our soul is breathed into our body, at which time we are made sensual, at once mercy and grace begin to work, having care of us and protecting us with pity and love, in which operation of the Holy Spirit forms in our faith the hope that we shall return up above to our substance, into the power of Christ, increased and fulfilled through the Holy Spirit. So I understand that our sensuality is founded in nature, in mercy and in grace, and this foundation enables us to receive gifts which lead us to endless life. For I saw very surely that our substance is in God, and I also saw that God is in our sensuality, for in the same instant and place in which our soul is made sensual, in the same instant and place exists the city of God, ordained for him from without beginning. He comes into this city and will never depart from it, for God is never out of the soul, in which he will dwell blessedly without end.

SELECTED BIBLIOGRAPHY

Baum, L. Frank, with pictures by W.W. Denslow. *The Wonderful Wizard of Oz*, George M. Hill Co., Chicago and New York, 1900.

Bellah, Robert N., et. al., *Habits of the Heart: Individualism and Commitment in American Life*, U. of California Press, Berkeley, 1985.

Bowe, Barbara, R.S.C.J., and Kathleen Hughes, R.S.C.J., Sharon Karam, R.S.C.J., Carolyn Osiek, R.S.C.J., *Silent Voices, Sacred Lives: Women's Readings for the Liturgical Year*, Paulist Press, Mahwah, NJ, 1992.

Cavanaugh, Brian, T.O.R., *Fresh Packet of Sower's Seeds*, Paulist Press, Mahwah, NJ, 1994.

Chilson, Richard, *Catholic Christianity, A Guide to the Way of the Truth and the Life*, Paulist Press, Mahwah, NJ, 1987.

Corry, Thomas M. *I Begin to See*, Long Run Productions, Santa Barbara, CA, 1990.

Csikszentmihalyi, Mihaly, *Flow, The Psychology of Optimal Experience*, Harper and Row, New York, 1990.

Dass, Ram, and Paul Groman, *How Can I Help?* Kroph Co., New York, 1987.

de Mello, Anthony, S.J., *Taking Flight, A Book of Story Meditations*, Doubleday, New York, 1988.

Dorff, Francis, O. Praem., *The Art of Passing Over, An Invitation to Living Creatively*, Paulist Press, Mahwah, NJ 1988.

Dulles, Avery, S.J., *A Church to Believe In, Discipleship and the Dynamics of Freedom*, Crossroad, New York, 1982.

———, *Models of the Church*, Doubleday, New York, 1974.

Farrell, Edward J., *Surprised by the Spirit*, Dimension Books, Denville, NJ, 1973.

Gjerding, Iben, and Kathrine Kinnamon, *Women's Prayer Services*, Twenty-Third Pub., Mystic, CT, 1983.

Greenleaf, Robert, *Servant Leadership, A Journey into the Nature of Legitimate Power and Greatness*, Paulist Press, New York, 1977.

Guzie, Tad, *The Book of Sacramental Basics*, Paulist Press, Ramsey, NJ, 1981.

Hall, Brian P., *The Genesis Effect*, Paulist Press, Mahwah, NJ, 1986.

Edward Hays, *Planetary Pilgrim*, Forest of Peace Books, Easton, KS, 1988.

———, *Pray all Ways*, Forest of Peace Books, Easton, KS, 1981.

———, *Prayers for the Domestic Church*, Forest of Peace Books, Easton, KS, 1979.

———, *St. George and the Dragon, and the Quest for the Holy Grail*, Forest of Peace Books, Easton, KS, 1986.

Kauzes, James M., and Barry Z. Posner, *Credibility, How Leaders Gain and Lose It, Why People Demand It*, Jossey Bass, San Francisco, 1993.

Loder, Ted, *Guerrillas of Grace, Prayers for the Battle*, Lura Media, San Diego, 1984.

Merton, Thomas, *Seeds of Contemplation*, Dell Publishing Company, New York, Copyright Our Lady of Gethsemani, 1949.

Muggeridge, Malcolm, *Something Beautiful for God, Mother Teresa of Calcutta*, Image Books, Garden City, NJ, 1971.

Palmer, Parker, *Stations of the Cross*.

Powell, John, S.J. *The Secret of Staying in Love,* Tabor Pub., Allen, Texas, 1974.

Powell, John, S.J., *Through Seasons of the Heart,* Tabor Pub., Allen, Texas, 1987.

Reiser, William, S.J., *The Potter's Touch,* Paulist Press, Ramsey, NJ, 1981.

Reutemann, Charles, F.S.C., *Let's Pray!,* St. Mary's Press, Winona, 1975.

————, *Let's Pray 2!,* St. Mary's Press, Winona, 1982.

Rock, Leo P., S.J., *Making Friends with Yourself, Christian Growth and Self-Acceptance,* Paulist Press, Mahwah, NJ, 1990.

Westley, Richard, *Good Things Happen, Experiencing Community in Small Groups,* Twenty-Third Pub., Mystic, CT, 1992.

————, *Redemptive Intimacy, A New Perspective for the Journey to Adult Faith,* Twenty-Third Pub., Mystic, CT, 1981.

Williams, Margery, *The Velveteen Rabbit,* Doubleday & Co, New York, 1970.

Fables of Aesop, The, Contemporary Books, Chicago, 1988.

National Organization Supporting Small Communities of Faith Buena Vista, Inc., P.O. Box 5474, Arvada, CO 80006-0474, 808-426-6622.

National Alliance for Parishes Restructuring Into Communities (NAPRC), P.O. Box 1152, Troy, MI 48099, 810-364-3500 (contact Sr. Geraldine).

North American Forum for Small Christian Communities (NAFSCC), Archdiosesan Office of Evangelization, 1935 Lewiston Drive, Louisville, KY 40216, 502-448-8581.